KU-048-540

Understanding
ADHD, Autism, Dyslexia and Dyspraxia

Professor Colin Terrell and Dr Terri Passenger

Published by Family Doctor Publications Limited
in association with the British Medical Association

IMPORTANT

This book is intended not as a substitute for personal medical advice but as a supplement to that advice for the patient who wishes to understand more about his or her condition.

Before taking any form of treatment
YOU SHOULD ALWAYS CONSULT YOUR MEDICAL PRACTITIONER.

In particular (without limit) you should note that advances in medical science occur rapidly and some information about drugs and treatment contained in this booklet may very soon be out of date.

© Family Doctor Publications 2005–2006
Updated 2006

Family Doctor Publications, PO Box 4664, Poole, Dorset BH15 1NN

ISBN-13: 978-1-903474-27-3
ISBN-10: 1-903474-27-2

Contents

About the authors

 **Professor Colin Terrell** is a Chartered Educational Psychologist working with young people and adults who have special educational needs. As a Senior Partner in a practice of educational psychologists, he works in their clinics in Harley Street and Nuffield Hospital, Cheltenham.

 **Dr Terri Passenger** is a Chartered Educational Psychologist working with children who have special educational needs. As a Senior Partner in a practice of educational psychologists, she splits her time between schools and the practice clinics in Harley Street and Nuffield Hospital, Cheltenham.

Introduction

What does this book cover?
This book describes the four most common disorders of childhood as follows.

Attention deficit hyperactivity disorder (ADHD)
Children with this condition have difficulty focusing their attention on an activity even for short periods, and often become overexcited and seemingly unable to control themselves.

Autistic spectrum disorder and Asperger's syndrome
Children with these conditions have difficulty developing and retaining social relationships with others, including children in their own age group, friends and other adults. They often have associated language disorders.

Specific learning difficulty (dyslexia)
Children with this condition have difficulty acquiring the skills of reading, spelling and writing at the same rate as other children in their age group.

Developmental coordination disorder (dyspraxia)

Children with this condition are slow to master tasks requiring motor coordination, for example learning to walk, learning to ride a bicycle, developing ball skills.

The basic features of each disorder – diagnosis, incidence and treatment strategies – are covered separately.

However, over the last decade, evidence has been accumulating that indicates that these particular disorders often occur in combination. Some child development specialists now believe that having two or more of these disorders together may be more common than just having a pure form of one of them.

All four disorders are covered in this single text. If you believe that a child known to you may show signs of one of these disorders, it may be helpful to read about all of them.

Attention deficit hyperactivity disorder

What is ADHD?

Medical research now suggests that attention deficit hyperactivity disorder (ADHD) affects different people in different ways and to different degrees of severity. There are a number of definitions but the following characteristics, generally accepted as the most common, are acknowledged in most definitions.

Children with ADHD are always 'on the go'; they:

- often talk incessantly

- frequently blurt out inappropriate comments

- often act impulsively

- rarely pause to think before they act

- sometimes endanger themselves by taking unnecessary risks.

These children are a major cause of concern to parents and teachers.

Who is to blame?

It is usually the parents who first suspect that there is something different about their child's behaviour. Many parents are embarrassed by their child's behaviour and often come to believe that they are largely to blame.

Research in recent years has, however, suggested that the bad or challenging behaviour displayed by some children is not the fault of their parents or the children themselves. It may be caused by inactivity in the areas of the brain that control concentration and impulsive behaviour.

When does it start?

The behaviours associated with ADHD become apparent during early childhood, before the age of five years.

ADHD is considered a lifelong condition but autobiographies of adults who had ADHD in childhood tend to agree that, although the 'symptoms' never go away, increasing maturity enables the individual to develop effective strategies that keep the behaviours in check.

Is there something wrong with my child?

Although parents sometimes sense that there is something 'not right' or uncontrollable about their child's behaviour, it is often an outsider, someone not in the immediate family, who is the first to suggest that a child might need specialist help. John's mother tells a typical story.

Case study: John

John's my second eldest so I only had his older sister to compare him with. I thought he was just like a boy should be – always rushing about like he was driven by a motor.

He couldn't stick at one thing for more than a few minutes and, even more worryingly, had no sense of danger. When we were out shopping, if I let go of his hand, he'd race out of the shop and be across the road in a flash.

He was four when he started at nursery and I still remember his teacher bringing him to me at the end of the first day, saying, 'He's a little terror isn't he?'. She wasn't joking; she meant it.

'John was always rushing about with no sense of danger.'

After the first week she spoke to me again and said that she didn't think he was ready for nursery. Apparently he'd bitten the cheek of one of the little girls because she wouldn't get out of a toy car he wanted, and then he'd kicked the nursery nurse who told him off.

We tried two other nurseries but the longest he lasted was two weeks.

When he started school, one or other of his teachers asked to speak to me about his behaviour almost every week. They said John seemed incapable of sitting still for more than a couple of minutes, was always shouting out answers in class, throwing tantrums and constantly quarrelling with other children.

We had trouble too whenever he was invited to parties. He'd just get so excited he was uncontrollable

'We tried two nurseries but the longest he lasted was two weeks.'

and it wasn't unusual for the parents running the party to ring up and ask me to collect him before the party was finished.

The problem with John and his behaviour came to a head when he was in his third year at junior school. We arrived at school a bit early one morning in the summer and, as usual, as soon as I let go of John's hand at the gate, he shot off straight away.

I started talking to some of the other mothers and about five minutes later there was this huge commotion in the playground. A small girl was on the ground, screaming, with blood pouring from a cut on her head.

'There was huge commotion in the playground; John had thrown a cricket bat across the playground, hitting a girl on the head.'

My heart sank because, in among the screaming, I could also hear John shouting and yelling. Apparently, he'd been playing cricket with some of the children and, just like always, when he was bowled out, John wouldn't let go of the bat and started shouting he wasn't out.

When one of the boys grabbed the bat, John had snatched it back and, shouting the others were cheating, had thrown it across the playground as hard as he could and it hit the girl on the head.

When I got to John he was completely out of control, still yelling that it was the other boy's fault and kicking and swearing at the teacher who was trying to hold him.

I managed to calm him down to the point where he stopped struggling and shouting and he started to cry, great big sobs, saying over and over again: 'I'm really sorry Mum, I didn't mean to hurt her. It wasn't my fault. I don't know why I do things like that. They all hate me. I wish I was dead.'

I took him home and he cried all day. What really upset me was that he kept on about how all the teachers and the other children hated him, how he'd never had any friends and how he wished he could kill himself. I'd never felt so down because I knew a lot of what he said was true.

The following morning I had an appointment to see the head teacher. He started by saying that, although he knew that John hadn't meant to hurt the little girl, there was a major problem with John's behaviour. It wasn't just what John did but how often he behaved badly.

Just before I left, he gave me a magazine from his coffee table, saying: 'I'm not an expert but I've seen kids like John before. He may have a problem he can't

'What really upset me was that he kept on about how all the teachers and other children hated him.'

'The head teacher gave me an article that described a boy with ADHD.'

help. Take a look at this page and see if you recognise John.'

I went straight home and read the article. It described a boy who'd been diagnosed with a clinical behaviour problem called attention deficit hyperactivity disorder (ADHD). The article described our John and even said what could be done. I can't tell you the relief that flooded over me.

The next day I took John to our family doctor and showed her the article and she arranged for John to be seen by a specialist. It took about six weeks for the appointment to come through but then, once John was diagnosed as having ADHD, things really started to look up.

'Once John was diagnosed as having ADHD, things really started to look up.'

The specialist gave us advice on how we could help him and he arranged for someone to go in to the school to give advice to the teachers. From that point whatever they did in school to handle John when he got excited we also did at home.

Believe me it wasn't easy, but that was seven years ago and John has just passed his GCSEs. He wants to be a PE teacher; the Careers Officer said he couldn't think of a better job for him!

What causes ADHD?

Precisely what causes ADHD is not yet known. However, it is generally accepted by medical experts that children are born with ADHD rather than developing it.

Evidence to support this comes from studies of children who have identical genetic make-up: identical twins. It has been found that, even if identical twins have been separated at birth and brought up apart, if one twin has ADHD the other twin will almost invariably have it too.

So, it is genetic make-up, not the way that the child is brought up, that seems to be the major factor in determining whether a child will suffer from ADHD. Further research evidence suggests that ADHD affects more boys than girls in a ratio of approximately four to one.

What is it like to have ADHD?
Overexcitement

Activities that, for other children, have relatively low levels of excitement are likely to overexcite a child with ADHD.

For example, waiting his turn to throw the dice in a board game will be difficult for him and he is likely to grab the dice, possibly unaware that this will annoy everyone else.

In the lunchtime queue at school, he may push past others to get his food as quickly as possible, again heedless of the fact that he'll lose friends and annoy lunchtime supervisors.

The child with ADHD sometimes talks incessantly, constantly interrupting others; his impulsive behaviour does not happen occasionally, but is a persistent and enduring characteristic, day after day.

Disliked

The ADHD child will, almost inevitably, be 'a pain' to everyone – members of his family, his teachers and last, but certainly not least, those who could be his friends.

The ADHD child is most often shunned by others of his own age because his unpredictable, impatient behaviour spoils games. When he is shunned, he is invariably sorry for what he has done.

Low self-esteem

The child or young adult with ADHD may, at times, look carefree and sometimes even 'devil may care'. However, the biographies of adults who have experienced this disorder in childhood often catalogue a series of unhappy memories.

They describe emotional distress, low self-esteem and loneliness, not being liked, being shunned by others, being persistently excluded from groups and banned from situations or activities in which they greatly wanted to participate.

An example of what it's like

To illustrate the problems of the ADHD child, let's take

Characteristics of a child with ADHD

Attention deficit hyperactivity disorder affects different people in different ways and to different degrees. However, the following chracteristics are most commonly found in children with ADHD:

- Often move more quickly into a state of high agitation or excitement than other children

- Often talk incessantly and loudly, are constantly moving and frequently switch from one activity to another without pause

- Cannot filter out unimportant stimuli – everything grabs their attention

- Annoy everybody and cannot help it

- Are disliked by others and realise this

- Have low self-esteem and often dislike themselves

- Are often remorseful after behaving 'badly', saying 'I can't help it'

- Demonstrate this behaviour in a persistent and enduring way

what you are doing right now as an example. Assume that you are reading this book in a relatively quiet room but are within earshot of a road where your car is parked alongside those of your neighbours.

A few seconds ago, you may have heard a car door slam but a part of your brain will have immediately filtered that noise out as normal and unimportant. You would, therefore, have been able to continue reading with your focus of attention uninterrupted.

Now assume that you hear a different sound, of crunching metal and tinkling glass. This time your filtering system identifies the sound as potentially significant and your reading will now be rapidly interrupted as you run to the window hoping your car is still in one piece!

In essence, one sound did not interrupt your train of thought because your brain 'unconsciously' filtered it out as 'unimportant' and you continued reading, yet another noise of roughly the same acoustic volume was not filtered out and caused you to interrupt your reading.

Now, as you are reading this book, sit quietly, try not to move and just listen to the noises around you. There may be a clock ticking, the low hum of a central heating or air-conditioning unit switching on, faint footsteps on the floor above, a muted burst of laughter from a television in a distant room.

For a minute or two close your eyes and just listen to the noises around you. Imagine that every time you hear any sound, it will completely interrupt your train of thought and divert your attention away from the book, towards the source of the sound.

Add to that all the other stimuli that your brain automatically filters out: inconsequential changes in light, temperature, touch, smell and sounds all have the potential to divert your attention.

In most cases, however, because you have an effective filtering system, the distractions that are relatively unimportant do not divert your attention. The child with ADHD does not have an effective filtering system, so each 'distraction' that his brain encounters has the same effect as that sound of crunching metal and tinkling glass may have had on you: it completely diverts his attention from a task.

Imagine then how such a child copes in a busy modern school with up to 30 other children in the same classroom and possibly hundreds of others in the school, all moving around the corridors and playgrounds. In such an environment, this child is likely to exhibit inappropriate behaviour by flitting his attention from one thing to another, distracting and annoying not only himself but also his fellow classmates and his teachers.

How is ADHD diagnosed?

In the UK, formal diagnosis of ADHD always requires specialist assessment by a paediatrician or a child/adolescent psychiatrist. However, the first point of contact should be with the child's family doctor who will need specific details of the behaviours that are of most concern.

If you think that a child may have ADHD, the screening questionnaire in the box on page 16 will help decide whether a referral to a medical specialist is warranted. Ideally, two adults who know the child well, usually a parent and a teacher, should complete the questionnaire independently.

How frequently is ADHD diagnosed?

The National Institute for Health and Clinical Excellence (NICE) is a group of experts who provide the government with advice on matters related to health. The NICE guidelines estimated that:

- About 1 in 100 of school-aged children manifests the most severe symptoms and acute difficulties associated with ADHD

- About 5 in 100 manifest less severe symptoms but nevertheless experience significant difficulties.

Screening questionnaire for ADHD

This questionnaire has been compiled to help you decide whether your child's beahviour shows enough of the characteristics of ADHD for a referral to a medical specialist to be warranted.

Before starting to complete the questionnaire, read the instructions below and follow them carefully.

Tick a box ONLY if BOTH of the following are true:

1. The child shows a particular behaviour to an excessive degree. (If you have to spend time thinking about your response then that aspect of the child's behaviour will probably not be excessive.)

   AND

2. The behaviour has been present since before the age of seven years and for at least the previous six months, and is present in different settings – for example, in school and at home.

Tick the box if the child often:

☐ fidgets with his hands and/or feet or squirms in his seat

☐ leaves his seat when being seated is expected (for example, at mealtimes)

☐ runs or climbs excessively in situations in which it is not appropriate

☐ has difficulties playing or engaging in leisure activities quietly

☐ appears 'on the go' and/or acts as if driven by a motor

☐ talks excessively

☐ blurts or shouts answers before questions have been completed

☐ has difficulty waiting turns in games, etc.

☐ interrupts or intrudes on others – for example, butts into conversations or games

If more than six behaviours are ticked then it is worth visiting your family doctor to discuss your child's behaviour.

This means, of course, that there are likely to be at least one or two children with ADHD in almost every school in the country.

What are the effects on families?

In the same report, the NICE noted that the knock-on effects for families who have an ADHD child can be very serious. In our culture, the parents of a child with ADHD will feel guilty about what they believe to be their own failure.

These feelings of guilt will often be reinforced by barely disguised negative comments and asides from relatives, friends, parents of other children, teachers, health professionals and even strangers in shops.

If a child with ADHD has a hard time, so do his parents. The pressure imposed on the parents and siblings of a child with ADHD can be so extreme that it can contribute significantly to family breakdown.

What can your doctor do?

From the completed questionnaire, your family doctor will have a good indication of the behaviours that are a particular cause for concern.

Once your family doctor has this information, she or he will usually begin the full assessment procedure by asking the advice of a range of specialists who might include a paediatrician, a child psychiatrist, an educational psychologist and your child's teachers.

These specialists will obviously seek information from you, as parents, because you are the adults who know the child best.

There is no one, single test for identifying ADHD so be prepared for the assessment process to take some time. Full reports on your child's medical history, family background and educational experience will probably be needed and it is likely that he or she will undergo a formal assessment, taking at least two hours, in a clinic as part of the referral to the paediatrician and/or the child psychiatrist.

How can my child be helped?

You will no doubt be relieved to learn that, if provided with appropriate treatment and sensitive skilled support, a child with ADHD can develop into a happy and successful adult.

However, living with a child with ADHD is not easy and you need to be reassured that many other parents also experience the frustration, tension and anxiety that you feel.

How to treat a child with ADHD is one of the most hotly contested debates in the media today and there are two major, and often opposing, schools of thought:

1   Those who believe that ADHD can be 'controlled' without medication – many of whom also believe that medication is simply 'wrong'.

2   Those who believe that the behaviours associated with ADHD can be effectively addressed with medication.

KEY POINTS

- Overactive or impulsive behaviour is shown at some time by most young children

- Overactive behaviour is not necessarily the fault of the child or parent

- A child's behaviour may not be within his control

- A child who is notable for excessive levels of activity may be suffering from a condition known as attention deficit hyperactivity disorder (ADHD)

- The exact causes of ADHD are unknown

- ADHD is thought to be genetic and unlikely to be caused by faulty upbringing

- ADHD affects more boys than girls in a ratio of approximately four to one

- If you are worried about your child's behaviour you should take him to your family doctor

- Your family doctor will need detailed information about the behaviours that worry you

- You may be referred to a team of specialists to assess your child fully

- Inform the school so that you can work together in arranging a full assessment

Assessment and management of ADHD

Non-medical treatment of ADHD
Diet and ADHD

Although there is no conclusive research evidence to support the idea that controlling a child's diet can influence behaviour, dietary intervention is often cited in media articles as a cause of ADHD.

The lack of conclusive evidence may simply be because such research is almost impossible to carry out in western society where most parents and children are fortunate enough to be surrounded by food.

Today, we live in a world where refrigerators are well stocked and unlocked, where shops and supermarkets are plentiful and practically always open, and where even the youngest member of the household can eat almost whatever he chooses at any time of the day – courtesy of the local home delivery or take-away service.

Stopping children eating particular foods or drinks is not easy. Therefore, the lack of any conclusive evidence linking diet and behaviour may simply suggest that such research is impossible.

However, some compelling anecdotal evidence for how diet can influence behaviour often comes from reports like this one, from Toby's dad.

Case study: Toby

Toby is our youngest son. Ever since he was born he seemed to be in a state of perpetual motion, into everything and could not be left alone for a minute. He was diagnosed with ADHD at the age of seven. By the time he was nine, life in the house was becoming unbearable.

We badly needed a break, but simply couldn't think what to do because on every previous holiday, hotel

'The other guests would complain about his behaviour.'

staff and other guests had complained about his behaviour. He was impossible to control in the dining rooms and was a positive danger to himself and others in crowded swimming pools.

So that year we decided to go on a walking holiday. Two weeks camping in the Yorkshire Dales, with no hotel staff or fellow guests to worry about.

The journey to Yorkshire was only 200 miles but it felt like 5,000: Toby was his usual irrepressible self – chaos in the car, needing to stop at every service station for a 'run-around' and then tearing round the tables and up and down the passageways. It's a wonder they didn't phone to warn the next service station he was on his way – or maybe they did?

On the first two days of the holiday he was as troublesome as ever but then, miraculously, he seemed

'The journey to Yorkshire was only 200 miles but it seemed like 5,000!'

'On the first two days of the holiday he was as troublesome as ever but then, miraculously, he seemed to calm down.'

to calm down, and the last ten days were ten of the best days we'd ever had with him.

Sadly, on the journey home, it seemed no sooner had we stopped for our first break at a service station, than Toby was back to his old self, shouting and racing about like a madman. When we eventually got home it was as if we'd never had a holiday at all.

A few days later I was talking about our holiday with my next door neighbour, a teacher, who suggested perhaps Toby's excitability had something to do with diet.

I have to admit I was a bit sceptical at first but she suggested we wrote down what Toby had eaten on the holiday.

When making out the list I realised that once we'd left all the service stations behind us, there just weren't any 'junk foods'. Almost by accident, Toby had lived for nearly two weeks with no burgers, no pizzas, no fizzy drinks. For lunch, we'd always had homemade sandwiches, which I'd filled with cheese or ham. In the evening we'd eaten at a little restaurant up the road from the campsite. On the first night, Toby had chosen Yorkshire gammon and onion-mash and liked it so much he had the same thing every night.

I decided right there and then to stop Toby eating junk food and for a week there were no burgers, pizzas or anything that could be called 'junk food' in the house. I gave Toby a packed lunch to take to school with strict instructions that he wasn't to eat anything else.

As you can imagine, all this caused a real pressure in the family because Toby's brother and sister weren't at all happy – they, of course, had grown to like their daily quota of burgers and pizzas. His sister said living with Toby was becoming 'a life sentence'.

In fact the whole diet thing nearly fell apart completely when, on the fourth day, Toby went to his cousin's party where, as a surprise for the birthday boy, everybody was taken to a burger-bar!

I was ready to give up at that point but at the start of the next week I decided banning burgers and pizzas was just too difficult so instead I banned every form of drink that had an additive: fizzy drinks, orange squash, milk-shakes, the lot. They could all have a burger, pizza, whatever – but no drinks with additives.

By Tuesday, the effect on Toby was miraculous. He was back to being like he was on the holiday. By Wednesday, when I picked him up from school, even one of his teachers mentioned the change in his behaviour.

'Even one of the teachers mentioned the change in his behaviour.'

On Friday he came home with a note saying what a good week he'd had and he had such a smile on his face! From that day on, Toby himself decided to take charge of what he drank.

This is a heartening story and there are many instances where parents have found that avoiding certain foods reduces challenging behaviour.

Which foods are commonly involved?

Chocolate and drinks with high levels of colourings, such as orange squash and colas, are frequently mentioned so you might first try eliminating these from your child's diet. If eliminating one or the other or both seems to improve your child's behaviour, test it out by noting his behaviour after he has resumed drinking them.

Finding the best diet by keeping careful records

If you want to examine whether there is a relationship between your child's diet and his behaviour, begin by keeping a fairly detailed record of your child's normal diet over a period of a few weeks – including everything, from the extra sugar on the cornflakes, to the cup of hot chocolate before bed.

At the same time, keep a record of your child's behaviour from day to day, perhaps scored on a scale of 1 to 5: where 1 means excellent behaviour, 3 means satisfactory behaviour and 5 means completely unacceptable behaviour. If possible give a separate score for morning, afternoon and evening.

It will probably be more convenient for you, as a parent, to keep the diary during part of a school holiday because it is not easy to keep a check on what a child eats at school: he can often buy some foods for lunch; friends will sometimes share sweets with him; and he may even 'swap' parts of the packed lunch that you so carefully prepared!

In addition, if you do need to keep a record of your child's diet and behaviour during term time, you will have to ask the school to help, for example, to keep a record of the child's behaviour. If this can't be done, then it's best to postpone the trial until one of the lengthier school holidays.

The record is likely to require more paperwork than you might at first think, as it is probably best to have a separate page for each day. The diary on page 27 is a very simplified example for one day.

Sample diary

Monday	Foods eaten	Behaviour	Notes
Morning	Cornflakes Milk Sugar Tea Toast Marmalade	1	Very good for most of morning. Helped Dad move grass cuttings from garden
Afternoon	Fish fingers Chipped potatoes Beans Crisps Fizzy orange juice Three chocolate biscuits	4	Very uptight, would not play sensibly with friends Not willing to wait turn in games
Evening	Cheese pizza Ice cream Chocolate sauce Tea Fizzy drink	5	Could not get him to sleep. Still awake at 2.00am

To help you find the best diet for your child you need to keep a careful record of what he or she eats and what his or her behaviour is like. To be useful it is probably best to have a page for each day as in this example.

Clearly, from the diary, behaviour was unacceptable both in the afternoon and in the evening. Before these episodes of unacceptable behaviour, the diary indicates that fizzy drinks and chocolate had been consumed.

Testing suspect foods

On subsequent days after the diary has been kept, you might try to arrange the diet so that neither of these items is present, and check consequent behaviour.

If behaviour seems improved when these two foods are eliminated, then you might reinsert fizzy drinks into the diet on one subsequent day and chocolate the next and note the result.

Using this method of systematic trial and careful record keeping, you can slowly attempt to find out which foods seem to be related to episodes of particularly unacceptable behaviour, and you can then try to eliminate these foods from the diet.

It should be noted that, for the purposes of this explanation, the diary has been deliberately simplified, and life is rarely this easy. It may take weeks of careful record keeping, together with systematic elimination

Finding the most appropriate diet for your child

- Keep a daily record of the food that your child eats

- Keep a daily record that 'rates' your child's behaviour through the day

- Examine both records to see if there are recurring instances where consumption of a particular food or drink seems to be followed by challenging behaviour

- When trying to eliminate suspect foods or drinks from your child's diet, make notes on what your child eats or drinks together with comments on his or her behaviour over the next few hours

- Before attempting to eliminate principal foods, such as wheat or dairy products, consult your family doctor

and reintroduction of particular foods, before clearly identifiable patterns emerge.

It is easy to be convinced by articles in newspapers and magazines, which suggest that so-called 'junk' foods and drinks are the *only* culprits. Toby's story (see earlier) is obviously a 'success' but there are many instances where eliminating 'junk foods' has not resulted in improvements in a child's behaviour.

Indeed, many parents have found their child's behaviour to be influenced by what are often thought to be 'good' foods, such as dairy or wheat products.

Getting expert advice
As a word of caution, if you are thinking of controlling your child's diet to any substantive degree, maybe by trying to avoid dairy or wheat products, you should consult your family doctor who may recommend that you speak to a dietitian.

What will it be like?
In real life, in a real family, this approach requires a huge commitment in terms of organisation, patience and persistence. Furthermore, it is unlikely that you will find a particular diet that 'cures all problems'.

It is more likely that avoiding certain foods may reduce challenging behaviour to a degree that makes family and school life more tolerable.

Behavioural programmes and ADHD
It is sometimes suggested that children with ADHD will benefit from what are called behavioural programmes. This means that a programme is devised that attempts to 'control' the child's behaviour by the systematic use of rewards.

The most successful behavioural programmes are those that involve both the parents and the school working together.

Case study: David

David is our second son; he's now aged 12, and we always had trouble with his behaviour almost from the day he was born. There've been frequent rows at home, and at school, always caused by David getting out of control and overexcited.

There're times when not me, his dad or his teachers can control him. Two or three times a term, the head teacher would telephone me to collect David from school because he'd become uncontrollable.

The school was patient with him for a long time but it all blew up into a big crisis when David was

'Two or three times a term the head teacher would telephone me to collect David from school because he had become uncontrollable.'

nine. He'd kicked his teacher when she tried to stop him running out of the classroom and we had a letter from the school saying David was suspended for five days and that if his behaviour didn't improve he'd be expelled for good.

The head teacher suggested that David be referred to a local child assessment unit and, as we were so worried he'd be permanently expelled from school, we agreed. As the assessment unit was part of the health service we needed a referral letter from our family doctor who provided it once we'd explained the problem.

About a month later David went to the assessment unit every day for a full week and, because the staff at the unit wanted details of David's behaviour almost from the time he was born, we also went for two afternoons.

In the week after the assessment, there was a case conference at David's school, which included us as David's parents, staff from the special unit, an educational psychologist and some of his teachers. The educational psychologist was there to help with what she called a 'behavioural programme', which would operate both at home and at school.

To be honest, the 'behavioural programme' all seemed a bit complicated at first and it took a few weeks for us and the school to work together, but once it got really started David gradually began to change for the better. Looking back, that meeting, and the help we had with the behavioural programme, was one of the best things that happened.

One of the conditions of the behavioural programme was that the school agreed to send a short report on David's behaviour home each day and, at the beginning of every school day, we sent a report back on his behaviour the previous night. This in itself had a big effect on David because he quickly realised that whatever happened at school we knew about it at home, and vice versa.

What really surprised my husband and me was how chuffed David was when he brought home school reports that said he had been good in some lessons. If he'd been no trouble in mathematics that morning we knew about it at home that night, and the same was true for all the other lessons. Obviously, there were lots of hiccups, because David still sort of 'lost it' sometimes at school, but there was usually more good than bad in the school reports.

'What really surprised my husband and me was how chuffed David was when he brought home school reports that said he had been good in some lessons.'

The educational psychologist said that both we and the school must be 'diligent throughout the day' in always letting him know immediately after he'd behaved well in a lesson, or after finishing a meal at home, or in getting ready for bed at the right time. (I admit I was so keen to do it properly, I even looked up 'diligent' in the dictionary to make sure we were doing it all just right!) The psychologist said it was important we didn't just wait until the end of the day to tell him he'd been a good boy.

With the help of the educational psychologist we and the school also had to work out a system of rewards and sanctions. For example, in school, after each lesson, David would either be given points for good behaviour or have points removed for bad behaviour. These would then be totted up throughout the day and David knew that when he got home then, depending on the number of points he'd earned, he'd have some kind of reward.

All the rewards were agreed with David in advance so he knew exactly where he stood. He always started a day with ten points, because if he had trouble in the first lesson he had 'minus' points and this just messed him up for the rest of the day. For example, if he came home and had 12 points he'd get extra time to use his Game-Boy and if he had 14 points he'd get more pocket money which we 'diligently' gave him each day rather than waiting until the end of the week.

If on a particular day he'd earned a lot of points, say 15 or more, he'd be allowed to save up some points for a special treat at the weekend, like being taken to the go-karting track which he loved. If David had fewer than 10 points at the end of a school day then we would cut down on the time he was allowed to spend at home on his Game-Boy or watching television.

The educational psychologist said it was very important that we were 'diligent', that word again, in making sure that the rewards were something David really valued and wanted. The rewards were not to be something *we* thought he wanted or that *we* thought might be good for him. This was sometimes quite hard for his dad because he didn't really like David watching too much television, which David loved.

In the beginning, one of the difficult parts of the programme was to convince David that the plan operated the same way both at school and at home in the sense that it wasn't just the school that gave or

'The rewards for good behaviour were things David really valued and wanted.'

took away points. We also did it at home, and at first David had difficulty accepting this because we'd never done anything like that before.

He's quite clever and, in the beginning, tried to make us feel guilty when we took away points at home. He complained that home was getting like school. In the end, though, I'm glad we stuck to the 'diligent' bit.

There were also times when David did something really, really bad and when this happened the educational psychologist said we'd have to operate a sanction, which was called 'time out'. This usually meant that David had to spend time alone in his room, without the television or his Game-Boy.

This was always for short periods and David always understood he could come out if he apologised in a way that showed he meant it, and was prepared to do as he was asked. His dad often used the phrase, 'he must apologise with good grace'. It's a bit of a strange way of putting it but David soon came to know what he meant.

The most difficult thing at home was stopping David arguing about how many points he should have if he did something good; he always wanted more. It was the same thing if he did something bad; he always argued that fewer points should be taken away.

The educational psychologist said it was very important we never argued or negotiated with David about how many points were to be given or taken away. This was always to be our decision, not David's, and if he argued we were told to subtract points, making it clear to him the points were being taken away just for arguing.

'The educational psychologist said that it was very important that we never argued or negotiated with David about how many points were to be given or taken away.'

It took David a few weeks to learn not to argue and, to be honest, it was also very hard for us not to join in when he did argue. We had to learn to be consistent, fair and always firm. Once David learned that arguing was pointless, and often even lost him more points, he stopped arguing. I have a sneaky feeling this was one of the best parts of the programme because, for the first time, David came to know that we, as parents, meant what we said.

We've been working this programme now for about 18 months. The details of the programme have to change periodically because the rewards have to change as David gets older: what is a reward one month may not be as effective as a reward next month.

I can't say everything's now perfect but life at home is certainly much easier and the reports from school indicate that his behaviour there has shown a huge improvement. The behaviour modification programme certainly hasn't been easy, not for David, and not for us his parents or the school, but things are much better now and in that sense it's worked and been worthwhile.

Medical treatment of ADHD
What drugs are given?

Guidelines issued in 2006 by the National Institute for Health and Clinical Excellence (NICE) recommend three alternative medications as appropriate treatments for children and adolescents with ADHD. The brand or proprietary and generic names for these medications are given in the box.

Brand name	Generic name
Ritalin	Methylphenidate
Strattera	Atomoxetine
Dexedrine	Dexamfetamine

Who prescribes them?

The guidelines issued by the NICE require that treatment with any of these medications be started only after a specialist who is an expert in ADHD has thoroughly assessed the child or adolescent and confirmed the diagnosis. Once treatment has been started it can be continued and monitored by a family doctor.

Ritalin

Of these three recommended medications Ritalin is the most commonly precribed and the brief explanation that follows gives the basic rationale for the use of Ritalin in the treatment of ADHD.

Exactly how Ritalin works is not known but it is thought to activate those areas of the brain that enable us to focus on a task. So Ritalin acts as a stimulant.

It does not, as the more alarmist sections of the media sometimes claim, turn children into non-thinking automatons. Medical research indicates that about 70 to 80 per cent of children with ADHD gain benefit from taking Ritalin.

Ritalin has the same effect on all people, not just an ADHD child. To understand its effects, it is perhaps worth noting that it is one of the most misused drugs among the college student population in the USA.

If a college student wishes to keep awake and study all night to prepare for an examination, Ritalin will help the student remain alert and focused, although, clearly, such misuse of Ritalin is both unwise and illegal.

Ritalin is not a cure for ADHD but, during the time that it is active, it allows the child to focus and control behaviour more effectively. Its effect lasts for about four hours, building up at the beginning and tailing off at the end, so it is generally at its most effective for the second and third hours of a four-hour period.

There is a long history of Ritalin being prescribed in tablet form, two or three times a day, which typically means that a child with ADHD would take one tablet between 8 and 9am to help with the morning session at school and then another at lunch time to help during the afternoon. In some cases he may need to take another tablet for the evening.

Are there any problems with medication?

Common problems with this form of treatment are, for example, that the child and/or carer might 'forget' to take the tablet, and some schools have proved to be wary of the legal situation in terms of non-medical staff (teachers) being responsible for the child taking the midday tablet.

However, medication is now more easily managed when the child is prescribed a 'slow-release' tablet, where he simply takes one tablet in the morning, rather than a tablet at intervals throughout the day. A recent survey has indicated that just over 50 per cent of Ritalin prescriptions are now for 'slow-release' tablets.

How long does treatment continue?

Treatment with methylphenidate (Ritalin) is normally considered a relatively long-term method of assisting the child with ADHD. It has already been mentioned that Ritalin does not 'cure' ADHD; it simply assists the child to control the symptoms.

It would not be possible to give a general rule on how long a child may be prescribed Ritalin, other than to say that it is taken for as long as the child needs it to control behaviour. As a result, treatment with Ritalin is often expected to operate over a period of years, as opposed to a few weeks or even months.

Regular review of medication

As with almost all medications some individuals may experience unwanted negative side effects, so 'good practice' demands that the effectiveness of the treatment be thoroughly monitored and reviewed regularly on the advice of the prescribing physician (most often a paediatrician).

A part of this review might, for example, require the child periodically to cease taking the medication for a short period to check that there remains a sufficiently marked increase in the behavioural symptoms associated with ADHD to justify continuing treatment with Ritalin.

Is Ritalin addictive?

Despite occasional statements reported in the media, Ritalin is not addictive, and there is little convincing evidence to indicate that it leads to any forms of addiction in later life.

Additional help with behaviour

Although Ritalin may help a child control unwanted behaviour, he may not know 'how' to behave because he has 'missed out' on the normal socialising experiences of childhood – such as how to behave with friends, how to join in conversations effectively, how to behave in the classroom and so on. Once started on a course of Ritalin it is almost as if the child needs a course in 'how to grow up quickly'.

The use of Ritalin should therefore be accompanied by a behavioural programme to help establish good strategies on how to behave. As shown in David's case study, ideally an educational psychologist (or other appropriately qualified medical/educational professional) will provide advice on the design of an appropriate behavioural programme.

Individual assessment

There is a great deal of controversy about the use of such medications and it is not possible to predict the length of time that a child may need to take them.

Each case must be carefully monitored by an appropriately qualified professional, usually a paediatrician or a child/adolescent psychiatrist.

Supporting a child with ADHD in school

As schools have access to advice from educational psychologists on how to manage a child with ADHD, the most sensible strategy is for the parents and the school to work together in supporting the child.

In addition to the points mentioned in the discussion of David's case study (see page 30), most schools try to ensure that the strategies in the box on page 42 are implemented and it is considered good practice that, where possible, the parents do likewise.

It can also help to pair the child with a good role model. However, it's important to remember that even the role model can't be perfect all the time!

Supporting a child with ADHD at home

Whether or not your child is treated with medication, you will be offered advice by a member of the specialist paediatric assessment team on strategies for managing your child's behaviour and helping him to control it. The following can help.

Rewards

The advice is likely to include some ideas on short-term reward systems, which are intended to offer your child an immediate reward for good behaviour. This is based on the theory that, for most human beings, behaviour that is rewarded is likely to be repeated, whereas behaviour that is ignored is less likely to be repeated.

Ten tips for effective child management in school

Schools tend to have the advice of educational psychologists on how to help a child with ADHD. The most sensible strategy is for the parents and the school to work together:

1 Ensure that every adult in the school understands the difficulties faced by a child with ADHD

2 In school, try to position the child close to an adult who can supervise his behaviour

3 Insist on eye contact when talking to the child and get him to repeat instructions

4 Give simple clear instructions; if necessary, break longer instructions into manageable chunks

5 Position the child away from obvious distractions (doors, windows, etc.)

6 Ensure that rewards are meaningful to the child and are given as often as is practicable

7 Remind the child that it is the *behaviour* (not the child) that is unwanted

8 Give firm reminders of what is needed and, when necessary, deal with correction in private

9 Ensure that there is no bargaining or prolonged discussion on what is or is not acceptable behaviour

10 Provide the child with a place of safety where he can retreat to calm down

Sanctions

You cannot always ignore challenging behaviour, however. There may be occasions when you have to operate some form of sanction. The most sensible is some 'time out' – which often means that the child has to spend some time alone in an allocated place of safety.

Time out

'Time out' should only be a short period, appropriate to the age of the child: a good 'rule of thumb' is one minute for each year of the child's age, so a five year old would have five minutes, an eight year old eight minutes, and so on. At the end of a 'time out', the child should be welcomed back with a smile, not with threats of further 'time outs'.

Be fair and consistent

The links between behaviour and reward must be made clear to the child and rewards and sanctions must be seen to be fair, just and consistent.

Developing an effective reward system

Nowadays, these behavioural management strategies, sometimes called 'behaviour modification', do not always involve the giving of material rewards such as sweets or more pocket money.

You will be encouraged to build up a repertoire of useful ways to indicate how pleased you are each time your child behaves well. This can be by giving verbal praise, or giving a hug, a thumbs-up sign or even in a less conspicuous style, such as a wink.

It is better to offer rewards and encouragement regularly and at short intervals rather than at longer

Points for parents to note about helping a child with ADHD

Behavioural management of a child with ADHD can give great benefit. Ritalin medication may also help. The following list summarises the main points:

- Adults must give instructions one at a time and clearly to the child

- Ideally, the child should be asked to repeat the instruction

- The child must be involved in identifying appropriate rewards

- The links between rewards and appropriate behaviour must be made clear to the child

- Equally, the links between sanctions and inappropriate behaviour must be made clear to the child

- Adults make decisions on the distribution of rewards and sanctions (there should be no bargaining)

- Rewards and sanctions are best handled within a structured routine that remains consistent – the child should know what to expect

- Adults must ensure that they are consistent and fair, but also firm

- Ideally schools and parents should work together on behaviour management

- A behavioural programme should involve both the home and the school

- An expert, such as an educational psychologist, should assist in developing the programme

Points for parents to note about helping a child with ADHD (contd)

- Any rewards must be 'valued' by the child (these are not always those preferred by parents and/or teachers)

- The programme must be operated in ways that are always consistent, fair and firm

- There should be no negotiation with the child concerning the issuing of rewards and/or sanctions; these are decisions made by the adults involved

- It's important to remember that overactive or impulsive behaviour is shown at some time by most young children

- Ritalin is a stimulant that enables a child to focus and sustain attention

- When Ritalin is properly prescribed and used, 70 to 80 per cent of ADHD children show improvements in behaviour

- Ritalin does not cure ADHD – it helps a child control behaviour

- Treatment with Ritalin is normally a relatively 'long-term' strategy with periodic reviews

- While on treatment with Ritalin the child will probably need help in learning how to behave appropriately

- Always remember that a child with ADHD is not showing challenging behaviour deliberately – it's no-one's fault

intervals. For example, in a very young child, ten minutes of good behaviour might be an appropriate interval to merit a reward whereas, in an older child, a reward every half-hour or hour may be more appropriate.

You may be given advice on using token systems, where your child is rewarded with tokens for good behaviour which he can swap for privileges such as watching some extra television or inviting a friend for a sleep-over.

Although it can be hard, it is important at all times to remind yourself that, although the behaviour is neither your fault nor your child's, he does need a consistent approach to help control it. So choose an approach that can be used by everyone: parents, grandparents, neighbours and teachers in school.

Any family with a child with ADHD is likely to be under great emotional pressure and will require skilled and sensitive support.

KEY POINTS

- Non-medical, dietary control may improve your child's behaviour

- Research evidence suggests that medication improves behaviour in 70 to 80 per cent of children with ADHD

- Parents and teachers should work together on strategies to modify behaviour in ADHD

- With appropriate support most ADHD children can and do grow up to be healthy, well-adjusted adults

Autistic spectrum disorder

What is an autistic spectrum disorder?

The word autism comes from two Greek words – 'aut' (meaning self) and 'ism' (meaning state) – and is used to define a person who is unusually absorbed in himself. Children with autistic spectrum disorder (often called ASD) have, in one form or another, difficulties in developing and retaining relationships with others.

The word 'spectrum' indicates that there is a wide variation in autistic behaviour along a spectrum from mild to severe. Autistic spectrum disorder is often described, by medical professionals, as a pervasive developmental disorder. This means that it affects *every area* of the child's everyday life.

Compared with this, a disorder such as dyslexia, although serious, tends to influence a child primarily in specific areas of everyday life such as reading, writing and spelling.

There are three elements to a diagnosis of autism and a child with autism will show *any or all* of the characteristics in the box on page 49.

Features of children with autistic spectrum disorder

There is a wide variation in autistic behaviour along a spectrum from mild to severe. It affects every area of life with the main difficulty being relationships with others. There are three elements to a diagnosis of autism – a child who is autistic will show any or all of the characteristics below:

1 Difficulties in using language to communicate with parents and other children – for example, a marked delay in the development of speech or speech limited to repetition with little sign of understanding

2 Difficulties in developing relationships with others – for example, there seems to be lack of awareness of others and reluctance either to make eye contact or to maintain it

3 Difficulties with pretend play and imagination – for example, prefers to be alone and play activities that are often unusually repetitive

The national media commonly mention two types: classic autism and Asperger's syndrome.

Classic autism

Classic autism is present when a child shows *all* three of the characteristics in the box above: the child has little or no language, does not seem to want to socialise with others and does not play like other children. The child also often has global learning difficulties which, in combination with his other difficulties, clearly and obviously impact on all aspects of his life.

Classic autism is considered to be at the more severe end of the autistic spectrum.

Asperger's syndrome

Asperger's syndrome is present when a child, at least in the first two or three years of childhood, appears to develop language relatively normally.

However, as the child's language develops, his speech shows unusual characteristics. He may develop an excellent vocabulary and can use speech to convey meaning accurately and well, but the flow and rhythm of his speech may sound robotic, stilted and unusually formal.

He also develops significant difficulties with the social aspects of language, which seriously affects the child's ability to form effective social relationships with adults or other children.

For example, during a conversation on a topic of interest to him, he may not recognise when others become bored or uninterested and persist with the conversation. He also may not realise that the truth may sometimes be hurtful, for instance, at a supermarket checkout, he might innocently point to the woman behind the till and say to his mother, 'She's very fat, isn't she?'.

To a child with Asperger's syndrome, such a comment is merely a statement of fact; he is not being deliberately rude, and will be completely unaware that the comment will be hurtful. He may also have difficulty appreciating humour.

Although the symptoms present in Asperger's syndrome influence almost all aspects of the life of the individual concerned, it is often considered to be at the milder end of the autistic spectrum.

The following two case studies illustrate the differences between classic autism and Asperger's syndrome.

Case study: classic autism

I remember the day that John was born; it was a home birth, just my husband Len and the midwife. My sister was downstairs looking after our other two children.

Everything was normal, John popped out no problem, and I still remember the midwife saying, 'He's a lovely little boy', as she cleaned him up and wrapped him in a sheet. The kids came up to see him, really excited they were, and we made a big fuss making sure they held him properly.

Things got back to as near normal as they can be in the next few weeks but when he was about two months old I noticed that John did not seem to act like his brother and sister had as babies.

'I remember the day that John was born. Everything was normal, John popped out no problem.'

'When he was about two months old I noticed that John did not seem to act like his brother and sister had as babies.'

He tended to lie motionless in his cot and his eyes didn't follow other people's movements yet some ordinary household noises, such as the vacuum cleaner, would cause him to scream and scream until they were switched off. He even cried when the woman next door used her vacuum cleaner which could only just be heard through the adjoining wall.

Although he learned to walk at the same time as my other kids he never learned to talk. He rarely made eye contact with anybody, not me, his father, his brother or his sister. He never reached out to be cuddled and when he was cuddled he seemed to dislike it and often tried to squirm away.

As he got older, he never asked for food or a drink or even pointed at what he wanted. When he cried, which he did a lot, I had to guess what he wanted.

He never pointed at things of interest, like when he first saw a horse or a cow in a field, he'd just looked at it. His brother and sister would have looked at it, then looked at me, then pointed to the horse, drawing my attention to it, making sure I saw it as well. John never did that, never seemed to want to share an interest in anything.

John would do simple things endlessly. All children learn that they can drop things but when John learned to drop things he did it over and over again. He would pick up one of his toy cars, drop it on the carpet, pick it up again, drop it again, and this could go on for hours.

'John would do simple things endlessly, hour after hour, day after day.'

At other times, he would hold the car in front of his eyes and spin one of the wheels, always the same wheel, always looking at it intently. Most children do things like this, but John would do it hour after hour, day after day.

He never seemed to want to play with his brother or sister, and ignored what they were doing. When I took him to nursery school he just curled up in a ball in a corner with his head on the floor, hands over his ears. Nobody could persuade him to join in any of the activities and, after four days, they asked me to take him away and he never went back.

He would often wake up in the night screaming for no apparent reason, and be inconsolable until he fell back into an exhausted sleep. He always woke up at

'When I took him to nursery school he just curled up in a ball in a corner with his head on the floor, hands over his ears.'

dawn, as soon as the room got light, and would lie in his bed staring fixedly at the small changes of light on the curtains.

As he got older, before going to infant school, he became very upset if any member of the family did not sit in exactly the same place at the table during meal times. At the table, he would eat only yoghurt, custard and jelly, nothing else. When normal foods like chips or meat were placed in John's mouth he immediately spat it all out as if just the 'feel' of some foods actually caused him pain.

He'd often try to eat things that other children would know were just plain wrong. Like when we took him to the seaside when he was six, he tried to drink

'At seven, he became fascinated by electric switches and fittings. Once I found him, fingers bleeding, fiddling with the bare wires of a bulb he had broken.'

the seawater and eat the sand. He'd try to eat things like newspapers and once tried to eat chunks of plastic he'd bitten off a computer disk.

At seven, he became fascinated by electric switches and fittings: if left alone he'd switch lights on and off for hours at a time. Even when light bulbs were hot he'd want to touch them, and often be crying with pain at the heat, moving his hand away but then almost immediately putting it back.

If his hand was moved from the bulb he'd often grab at it again, so fast that on one occasion he shattered the glass and cut himself. Another time I found him, fingers bleeding, fiddling with the bare wires of a bulb he had broken on a bedside lamp.

'Going to the special unit for children with autism has made a big difference. Although progress is slow it seems to be working.'

By the time he was seven, I knew something was seriously wrong, but I didn't want to believe it. I wanted to believe what everybody said, 'Be patient, he's just a bit slow that's all, he'll grow out of it'.

The school couldn't cope any more, even though he had a classroom assistant with him virtually all the time. They suggested that he be assessed and he now attends a special unit for children with autism attached to a junior school.

Going to the unit has made a big difference. The way they treat him at school we try to do at home and although it's slow it seems to be working.

He's nine now and just the other day, when his father came in the room, he looked up and for the first time said, 'Daddy back'. Not a big deal for most children, but a giant step for us.

Case study: 'Asperger's syndrome'

James is my only child; he was born in Germany when my husband was in the forces. We came back to the UK when James was five and he started at the local primary school. After the first few days the first thing his teacher said to me was, 'He's got a fantastic vocabulary hasn't he?', and he had.

The trouble was he just didn't seem to get on with other children, or rather they did not get on with him. The problem was that, although he really wanted to mix, he always needed to take charge, almost like he thought he was the teacher.

James tended to speak to the other children in an 'adult way', telling them off when he thought they were being naughty, and when he told them off he'd use words and a tone of voice that was just like the head teacher.

If you didn't know him, you'd sometimes think he was 'taking the Mick' out of the head teacher, but he wasn't, it was just the way James talked. He didn't seem to realise the other kids didn't like it.

There's a lot of things about James that make him different. For example, he's always been, and still is, very fussy about how he dresses and what he wears. He always insists on the same clothes, and always puts them on in exactly the same order.

Dressing in the morning is like following a ritual; he gets very upset if things aren't exactly right. If, for some reason, we can't find his school shoes he won't wear a substitute pair, because James will just say 'they're not the right colour black', and he means it.

'James tended to speak to other children in an adult way, telling them off when he thought they had been naughty.'

In junior school, there were times when the way he spoke caused teachers to think he was rude, the joker of the class. On one occasion, at the end of an art lesson, a teacher said, 'OK class, shall we clear up now?'.

The teacher used a tone of voice that all the other children recognised as an instruction, not a question. But James had simply shouted out 'No' and carried on painting. When the teacher spoke to him later James just couldn't understand that he'd done anything wrong; as far as he was concerned he'd just answered the question.

On another occasion, when a teacher asked him, 'Do you know the time?' James simply answered the question, 'Yes', and had no idea why the teacher accused him of being 'a rude boy'.

'Dressing in the morning is like following a ritual; he gets very upset if things aren't exactly right.'

Although James understands the literal meaning of words and sentences, he does not seem to understand that sometimes the literal meaning is not what is actually meant.

I remember, when he was very young, he repeated a swear word he'd heard on television to his Granny. James really likes her, and will do anything for her, so when she'd innocently snapped, 'Bite your tongue young man', that's exactly what he did.

If he's being a bit slow and we say, 'Come on James, pull your socks up', the likely result is that James will actually reach down and pull up his socks.

He never seems to understand either that 'the truth' can really upset others. On one occasion, at a school assembly a teacher had put his hand to his ear and shouted above the noise, 'Can I hear somebody talking?'.

Everybody, even the infants, knew what the teacher meant; it was simply a way of asking for everybody to quieten down. But not James; above the slowly reducing noise he'd instantly yelled back, 'Yes, sir, it's Jonathan, Simon and Mark'.

As a result of the way he talks, and what he says, James has always been bullied; it's a major problem, but even I can understand how the other children feel, and why they pick on him, but James, he hasn't got a clue.

When he was eight, he became interested in 'Star Wars', but it went beyond interest and became an obsession. Everywhere he went James insisted on taking his seven Star Wars books with him, to school, visiting relatives, even going shopping. They were so bulky he had them in a small rucksack.

And if he couldn't find one of them he wouldn't leave the house, even if he was just going swimming.

'As a result of the way he talks, and what he says, James has always been bullied and teased.'

He would, if unchecked, keep a Star Wars monologue going for an hour or more. Adults frequently had to ask him to stop talking, whereas his classmates simply made fun of him or avoided his company.

When he began collecting car numbers life literally became unbearable. For months and months, every evening in the summer and at weekends, he'd go down to the corner of our street and sit on the pavement writing down the registration number of every vehicle that passed.

He even had different books for cars, lorries, vans, buses and motorbikes. He'd fill in book after book, for no apparent purpose other than collecting the numbers. And if you'd let him, he'd talk about them for hours, pointing out interesting numbers.

At the age of 12 years, James was diagnosed with Asperger's syndrome and a special teacher now visits

'When he started collecting car numbers life literally became unbearable.'

the school to work with him and give advice to his teachers. I must say things have improved.

The teachers now seem to accept him more and there are fewer misunderstandings about some of the things he says, and how he says things. They've also got to grips with the bullying and James now quite likes going to school.

What are the everyday signs of an autistic spectrum disorder?

As mentioned earlier, children with autistic spectrum disorders experience difficulty in one or more of three areas of behaviour. Examples are given in the box on pages 64–5 of everyday instances of autistic behaviour under each of the three major headings.

Tick the box if your child *persistently* shows the behaviour. If you have to think hard about any one of the questions, then your child probably does not show the behaviour to a degree that warrants ticking the box and the answer is probably 'no'.

If one or more items are ticked under two or more headings then it is worth visiting your family doctor to discuss possible referral to a paediatrician for a more comprehensive assessment.

Causes, incidence and long-term consequences of autism
Causes

The exact causes of autism are not fully understood. Medical evidence suggests that children are born with autism rather than developing it during childhood.

It is generally accepted that autism has a biological basis but it is not yet clear whether it results from a chemical imbalance, or an anatomical or physiological brain difference. There is, however, compelling evidence of a strong genetic component.

It is important to stress that there is no research evidence to indicate that autism is in any way linked to inappropriate or inadequate parenting.

There is also no substantive evidence that environmental factors, such as fetal development in the womb, difficulties at birth, childhood diet, immunisation, infantile injury and pollution, are primary factors in the cause of autism.

However, almost all of these factors have been suggested as possible causes and each has periodically attracted huge media attention, but with very little research evidence to back up the claims.

Everyday signs of autism

Children with autism show difficulty with one or more of three areas of behaviour. The list below gives everyday examples of typical difficulties in each of the three areas. Tick the box if you think the example describes your child's behaviour.

Spoken language and communication

Tick the box if your child:

☐ Failed to develop spoken language by an appropriate age and does not attempt to compensate with non-verbal communication – for example, smiling at others, pointing to a cupboard where sweets are kept

☐ Shows a marked difficulty in communicating with other children and adults – for example, initiating or sustaining conversation, holding out a hand when help is required, demonstrating wishes or responding by nodding or shaking his head

☐ Repeats the same words or phrases, sometimes at the wrong time, the wrong place or to the wrong audience – for example, saying 'shut up' to an adult

☐ Has failed to learn by imitating and/or communicating with others – for example, parents or other children – and does not engage in make-believe play – for example, pretending to drive a car like his parents or pretending to make a cup of tea and drink out of an imaginary cup

Relationships with others

Tick the box if your child:

☐ Fails to make eye contact easily and/or does not use facial expressions appropriately – for example, smiling to show that he or she enjoys the company of others

Everyday signs of autism (contd)

☐ Does not seem able to develop relationships with other children of the same age

☐ Does not seem to share activities or interests with other children; is often alone even when other children are around – as in playgrounds or at birthday parties

☐ Does not want to participate in give-and-take activities with other children – for example, letting others borrow a favourite toy, or turn-taking in a game

Play and imagination

Tick the box if your child:

☐ Often prefers to play alone and appears preoccupied with one or more repetitive activities for a longer period than might be reasonably expected – for example, turning a light switch on and off, picking up and dropping an object

☐ Insists on sameness and routine – for example, dislikes changes such as surprise visits to the cinema or the swimming pool, always wants to watch the same video from beginning to end

☐ Frequently flaps his hands and/or fingers, spins on the spot or rocks backwards and forwards

☐ Is often over-interested in part of an object rather than the object – for example, the wheels of toy cars not the car, the tops of jars or ketchup bottles, the key in a door

Incidence

Autism is present in all social classes, races and cultures. Although it is possible to diagnose autism by about the age of 18 months, in practice the diagnosis is rarely made until after 24 months and the average age of diagnosis is 5 years.

The actual incidence of autism is hotly debated. This is mainly because some surveys attempt to identify only cases of classic (severe) autism and consequently come up with relatively low estimates. Other surveys have used less strict criteria and include children who show some of the signs of autism – for example, including children with Asperger's syndrome – and so the numbers of children said to be autistic will be higher.

In 2001, the Medical Research Council published a review of autism in children aged up to eight years in the UK. The report found that approximately:

- 1 to 3 children per 1,000 show 'severe autism'
- 6 children in 1,000 show 'some signs of autism'
- more boys than girls show autism, in the ratio of approximately 4 to 1.

On the basis of the above findings it can be expected that most mainstream infant and junior schools in the UK will have one or more pupils with some degree of autism.

In terms of whether autism is occurring more frequently nowadays, it is difficult to be sure for two main reasons:

1 Over the last 5 to 10 years autism has become better known than in the previous 50 years. Parents, medical professionals and teachers are now far more aware of autism and so much more likely to suspect or

diagnose it. This has probably contributed, over the last two decades, to the steady increase in the number of children diagnosed as showing autism. However, this does not mean there has been a *real* increase in autism; it may just be more frequently diagnosed.

2 Symptoms of autism are often 'fuzzy'. For example, the judgement of one clinician varies from another, so a symptom such as 'lack of eye contact' may be attributed to autism or to something else, such as 'extreme shyness'. The same applies to many of the other symptoms of autism – for example, 'prefers to play alone', 'does not engage in make believe play'. There is no exact point at which such symptoms move from the low end of the average range of personality characteristics to clinical dysfunction.

Long-term consequences

There is general consensus that autism is a life-long condition and, to date, there is no credible research evidence that autism can be cured. Long-term studies indicate that those diagnosed with autism will continue to experience the features associated with it throughout their lives.

However, there is good evidence to indicate that the symptoms can be lessened, in the sense that the child with autism and the family can be helped to cope.

Some children with autism (particularly those diagnosed as having Asperger's syndrome) may go on to live independent adult lives and may themselves have partners and their own children. Others may live semi-independently, with support from their families and Social Services. A minority will live in specialist accommodation for those with autistic spectrum disorders.

What does it feel like to be a child with autism?

In cases of severe or classic autism, it is not possible for such a child (or adult) to explain how he feels so we can't know what it is like for him.

In their own world

Many professionals think that these individuals see and experience the world in such a unique way that it is incomprehensible to the non-autistic person.

According to this view, children who are autistic should be cared for rather than educated. This means that, if a child with autism seems happy in his world, it would be unethical to force him to accept the non-autistic view of the world as in some way correct and better.

Unhappy

There is a wealth of anecdotal or autobiographical accounts of what it feels like to be 'autistic' from those able to communicate – mainly those who have Asperger's syndrome. These accounts generally catalogue unhappy childhoods full of misunderstandings caused by the difficulties with social communication.

It helps to find a niche

Those who have the condition and who claim to have overcome their unhappiness have generally successfully channelled their obsessive behaviour into some form of career. For example, one famous modern artist, Lucien Freud, was recently diagnosed as having Asperger's syndrome. He acknowledges that, as an obsessive painter who rarely engages in any other activity, he is highly successful.

Some very famous scientists may also have shown signs of relatively mild autism or Asperger's syndrome – for example, Isaac Newton, Albert Einstein and Marie Curie. The painter J.M.W. Turner is now thought to have shown signs of Asperger's syndrome as did the composer Bela Bartock and the philosopher Ludwig Wittgenstein. All these individuals experienced difficulties in socialising with others and had obsessional interests.

Strengths

It is worth noting that children with mild autism and/or Asperger's syndrome often have particular strengths in terms of their ability to:

- learn by rote

- develop a very wide vocabulary

- focus extensively (and sometimes exclusively) on a particular hobby or interest which is often more technical or scientifically based than the hobbies of his peer group.

It is sometimes whimsically noted that many of our universities are filled with academics who display mild autistic traits in terms of their 'obsessional' interest in a specific subject area!

What is it like for parents?

No discussion of autism would be complete without mentioning the feelings of parents who are charged with the responsibility of raising a child with autism. This is a particularly difficult task, especially if the child appears to behave in ways indicating that he is unaware of the care that the parent is persistently offering. Living with a child with autism is not easy.

KEY POINTS

■ The exact causes of autism are unknown but children are born with autism, it is not caused by poor parenting

■ It is helpful to distinguish between at least two types of autistic spectrum disorder: classic autism and Asperger's syndrome

■ The child with 'classic' autism displays *all* three of the major signs of autism and has difficulties with language and communication, social relationships and imaginative play, and often has obsessive interests and/or indulges in repetitive behaviours

■ The child with Asperger's syndrome may have difficulties in the social aspects of language such as appreciation of humour, and tends to use rather more formal or pedantic speech than other children of his own age

■ These difficulties pervade every aspect of the child's everyday life

Assessment and management of ASD

Medical treatment

There are no specific medications available for the treatment of an autistic spectrum disorder (ASD), although drugs are sometimes used to control one or other of the symptoms of autism. For example, Ritalin (the brand or proprietary name for the drug methylphenidate) is sometimes prescribed to help a child focus attention.

One British government survey identified 17 different treatments for autism, all of which could be described as behaviourally based or non-medical treatments.

Non-medical treatment

When discussing non-medical interventions it is perhaps worth noting that most of them could perhaps be more approriately termed 'educational programmes' than 'treatments'. All are very different but have one common feature in that they aim to help children with autism cope better with their difficulties.

Behavioural programmes

Behavioural programmes for autism vary greatly in complexity and there is surprisingly little *research evidence* on the success or otherwise of these, but this does not mean that they do not work. Justification for each 'treatment' method often comes from anecdotal evidence, usually in the form of testimonies from parents.

The programmes also vary greatly in their intensity: some are delivered during almost all waking hours with an almost continuous one-adult-to-one-child set-up. Other programmes are simpler and less intensive – for example, working through a series of specifically written 'social' stories that offer advice to a child with autism on how to behave appropriately and so become more integrated into family life and other social settings.

It is generally accepted that the earlier a behavioural programme is started (some experts say as early as 18 months), the greater the chance of success. The choice of programme is often determined by the severity of the autism and the preferences of the family. The best results are found when a consistent approach is adopted by all adults interacting with the child.

Brief descriptions of four very different but often used treatment programmes are given below to illustrate the range and diversity of options.

Applied behaviour analysis

Applied behaviour analysis (ABA) is based on the principle that behaviour that is rewarded is more likely to be repeated than behaviour that is ignored.

When a child with autism uses appropriate behaviour, such as initiating a communication with another person, even in the form of a fleeting glance or the briefest of smiles, it is rewarded in the hope that it will be repeated and ultimately become commonplace for that particular child. Behaviour that is inappropriate, such as the child failing to initiate any form of contact, is ignored.

A simple example

To see how it is done, let's assume that a child likes potato chips (french fries) but does not yet use a fork at the table. The task is to teach the child to use a fork.

The adult teaching the child might begin by first sitting in front of the child with just two or three potato chips on a plate plus a fork. The adult will wait until the child makes eye contact (initiates a contact) and the adult will then eat a chip using the fork (a demonstration). The adult will then place the fork in the child's hand, spear a chip and guide the child's hand to his mouth (a reward).

Once the child has compliantly cooperated in these actions a few times, the adult will place the fork in the child's hand, help him spear a chip, but then wait for him to lift the fork to his mouth without further assistance. The next step will be for the child independently to pick up the fork, spear a chip and lift it to his mouth.

This example gives a basic idea of what happens but there are often many more steps than described here. The process of learning to eat with a fork can extend over a period of days, weeks, months or even years.

How it's done

To apply the ABA method, a complex skill such as using a fork is broken down into small steps. Each of these small steps is described as a 'discrete trial'.

Complex life tasks such as toilet training, dressing, making requests for specific drinks and food are all broken down into discrete trials and taught to the child using appropriate rewards.

ABA treatment is a highly intensive approach. Children usually follow the programme for 30 to 40 hours a week, one to one, with a series of trained professionals on a rotating shift basis.

Over a period of years all basic life tasks are taught in discrete steps and the child masters each task using the principle of rewarding appropriate behaviour and ignoring less appropriate behaviour.

Is it effective?

This method is not without controversy. Some practitioners feel that it is emotionally too difficult for a child with autism, that the time requirement of 30 to 40 hours a week is too intensive and intrusive on family life, and that, although it may change a particular behaviour, it does not prepare a child with autism to respond to new situations.

However, although there is no substantive research evidence to indicate that this technique is successful, there is an abundance of anecdotal evidence from parents of its effectiveness in teaching new skills and behaviours to children with severe autism.

TEACCH

This style of intervention was first developed in the USA and its full title is 'Treatment and Education of Autistic and Communication Handicapped Children' or, as is more commonly known, the TEACCH system.

As it both recommends focusing on the needs of the child with autism and demands a structure to the learning environment (predominantly visual) that suits the child, it is used more often in special schools or units, although it is sometimes adapted for use in normal schools.

The following example provides a description of the basics of the TEACCH approach.

An example of TEACCH in action

Abigail is a child with autism aged seven who, when placed in a normal infant classroom, showed high levels of anxiety. In such classrooms up to 30 pupils are often moving from one task to another, children are quite rightly encouraged to talk to each other and to teachers, the walls are filled with exciting materials designed to be 'eye catching' and there is an almost constant level of noise and activity.

Abigail found life in such a classroom so persistently frightening that she was transferred to a less anxiety-provoking classroom in a special school that operated the TEACCH system.

Ideally, a typical TEACCH classroom will have perhaps four to six children with one teacher and a learning support assistant. The particular classroom activities and the order in which Abigail has to do them will be shown on a 'visual timetable' or list of pictures displayed on the wall.

The classroom itself will be relatively 'plain' with no distracting wall displays and there will be a set place or workstation for each of the different class activities. Each workstation will have a tray in which will be the exercises that Abigail is expected to complete during that day and another separate tray for her completed work.

When an activity is finished Abigail will be expected to move to the next activity on the visual list. This insistence on set routines for virtually every classroom activity is designed to reduce Abigail's levels of anxiety.

The TEACCH strategy also places emphasis on a high level of cooperation between school and home in that the principles designed to reduce Abigail's classroom anxieties will be, where possible, mirrored at home. Abigail may, for example, have a list of visual cues to forewarn her when she is expected to clean her teeth, when she is expected to begin dressing, when she is expected to eat lunch, and so on.

The TEACCH system tries to modify both home and school environments to fit the needs of the child with autism, rather than expecting the child with autism to fit into what could be called the 'normal' demands of home and school.

Picture Exchange Communication System

One of the main areas affected by autism is the ability to communicate, particularly using spoken language. Some children with autism develop a limited degree of verbal language, whereas others may never talk.

The Picture Exchange Communication System (PECS) is a simple communication programme used in many specialist schools to get language started as well as to provide an ongoing way of communicating for those children who may never talk. If a child with autism is unlikely to use verbal communication effectively, he may be able to learn to use a simple set of pictures. Below is an example of how the PECS is used.

A simple example

A child carries around some simple pictures showing certain activities. They may be a glass and a bottle, a toilet, a child's playground swing. Each drawing is about the size of a playing card and a set of them is often held together at the corner by a keyring.

Children will be expected to show an adult an appropriate picture instead of talking – such as the picture of the swing if they want to go out to play, the picture of the toilet if they wish to use it, the glass and bottle if they are thirsty.

Clearly, each time a 'picture' is exchanged the adult will 'say' the word and encourage the child to do likewise. Hopefully, the child will eventually use the correct word each time a picture is exchanged until, eventually, the child will be able to use particular words on his own to make requests, instead of pictures.

Advantages

The advantage of the PECS is that, when a request is made, it is clear, intentional and, most importantly in the case of a child with autism, *initiated by the child*. The child hands the adult a picture, and his request is immediately understood.

It also makes it easy for the child with autism to communicate with anyone – all he has to do is accept the picture. Clearly, there is a need for coordination and consistency in the use of pictures both at home and at school.

Social stories

Social stories were developed for teaching social skills to children with autism, mainly children with Asperger's syndrome. The approach focuses on 'theory of mind' deficits – a lack of ability to understand or recognise the feelings, points of view or plans of others.

A relatively simple way of explaining this is to describe one of the techniques commonly used to assess whether a child with autism has a theory of mind.

An autistic child's theory of mind

A child with autism is shown a tube of Smarties (the children's sweets in the distinctive wrapper) and is asked, 'What is in the tube?'. The child will normally say 'Smarties'.

The adult then opens the tube and shows the child that this tube actually holds a red pencil. The adult then places the pencil back in the tube and then asks the child, 'If your mother saw this tube what would she think was in it?'.

Most children would now respond that their mother would think it was full of Smarties, because they are able to see the situation from the mind of their mother. A child with autism can see the situation only from his point of view and is likely to say that his mother would think there is a red pencil in the tube.

Stories to develop a child's theory of mind

An essential requirement for developing effective social relationships is that a person must at times be aware of what others may be thinking (they may be bored, upset, happy, sad, angry) and react appropriately. Social stories are descriptions of particular social interactions and help to give a child with autism and/or Asperger's syndrome enough information to help him understand others' points of view.

The stories typically have three sentence types:

1 Descriptive sentences, which address the 'where', 'who', 'what' and 'why' of a situation.

2 Perspective sentences, which give some understanding of the thoughts and emotions of others.

3 Directive sentences, which suggest a suitable response.

These stories frequently incorporate pictures, photographs or music. Some published versions of social stories are available but they can be written by anyone living or working with the child and personalised to address the social situations that are most difficult for each particular child.

Which treatment?

The examples of treatments given above demonstrate that programmes range from highly intensive, involving most waking hours, to ones that are considerably less intensive: the ABA affects every aspect of a child's life; the PECS is a useful addition to a child's communication skills but need not necessarily dominate life; social stories will be used only in special lessons during the week.

What will be appropriate for one child or family may not be appropriate for another. The choice of treatment programme will depend on a range of factors such as the severity of the autism and the resources available to a particular family.

KEY POINTS

■ The earlier that treatment is started the greater the level of success

■ Most treatments are educational rather than medical

■ Treatment works best if consistent across different settings – parents, carers, therapists

Dyslexia

What is dyslexia?

The British Psychological Society defines dyslexia as:

> … evident when accurate and fluent word reading and/or spelling develops incompletely or with great difficulty.

This indicates that, although people with dyslexia can learn to read and spell, they will do so with difficulty.

What is it like to have dyslexia?

One of the most common activities for a class of children is to be asked to read a task from a white board, a class worksheet or a textbook, and then to write something in an exercise book. Every day in the classroom, in lesson after lesson, children with dyslexia see their friends completing such tasks with apparent ease, yet they find such tasks very difficult.

It is not surprising that many of them, in addition to having difficulty with reading and spelling, also lose their sense of self-esteem and may even come to believe that they must be stupid.

The following account by Emily's mother illustrates the problem.

Case study: Emily

Emily was an easy baby. There was no difficulty with feeding and she was soon sleeping all through the night, not like her elder brother who seemed to want feeding every two hours, night and day.

Emily did all the right things at the right time, sitting up, crawling and walking but, although she had no difficulty understanding what was said to her, she sometimes seemed to have difficulty getting her words out clearly. She'd say things like 'par-cark' for 'car-park' or 'poppotomus' for long words like 'hippopotamus'. It became a family joke and her older brother and sister teased her about it.

'She had no difficulty understanding what was said to her, but she sometimes seemed to have difficulty getting her words out clearly.'

When she started infant school, all the teachers liked her. They said that in class she was 'brighter' than most of the other kids at answering questions but she just couldn't seem to learn things that involved what the school called 'rote' learning. That's things like learning to say the alphabet, the days of the week and the months of the year, things that were really just long series of sounds.

The real problems began when she had to learn the sounds linked with letters, things like the letter 'b' represents the sound /buh/ and the 'c' a /cuh/ sound. We spent hours at home trying to help her, but she couldn't seem to learn.

She was brilliant at telling a story about something that had happened at school among her friends and was better at jigsaws and Lego than her older brother, but she couldn't get the hang of even simple things to do with reading and writing.

As she moved up to juniors, she went through periods of being very unhappy because her friends were all reading and writing things at a much higher level than her. As the years went by the gap just got bigger and bigger and she slipped further and further behind.

Things like homework became very difficult. She couldn't copy the instructions from the white-board quick enough so I often had to ring her friends' parents to find out what she was supposed to do. She started to say there was no homework, which wasn't true, but she found it so difficult, we had tears night after night.

There were some things she was really good at. One Christmas, a local toy manufacturer sponsored a competition. The prize was a computer for the school that produced the best homemade toy.

'As the years went by the gap just got bigger and bigger and she slipped further and further behind. Things like homework became very difficult.'

Emily made a joke Paddington Bear look-a-like; she dressed him like a 'Hell's Angel'. Instead of a navy cloth duffle coat and red hat, he had long hair in a pony tail, a fierce looking eye patch, black T-shirt and torn jeans. Just looking at it made you smile. Emily was the winner in her age range; it was even put on show in one of the local toy shops.

When she was about ten, I think it was in Year 5, the junior school asked me if I would let an educational psychologist see her for an assessment. I wasn't happy about it because I thought 'psychologist', that sounds serious, but I agreed because by that time I was so worried.

After the assessment, the psychologist wrote a report that said Emily's intelligence was above average but she had a specific difficulty with reading and writing. She said the correct term was 'specific learning

'There were some things she was really good at. One Christmas she made a "Hell's Angel" teddy bear that won first prize in a competition.'

difficulties (dyslexia)' and explained that it meant exactly what it said: Emily was bright enough to learn almost everything as well as everybody else, she just had a specific difficulty with reading and writing.

The report also said there were things that could be done about it and, wow, what a relief that was, for me and for Emily.

The school and the psychologist arranged for a specialist dyslexia teacher to see Emily for 30 minutes one-to-one teaching on a Tuesday and a Thursday. The specialist gave advice to Emily's class teachers on how to help her cope better in the classroom and with homework.

Over the next few months, Emily's reading and writing began to improve, her confidence came back and she stopped saying she was 'thick'.

'The school and psychologist arranged for a specialist dyslexia
teacher to see Emily for 30 minutes twice a week.'

She had help right through junior and secondary
school, always just for short periods during the week.
The secondary school arranged for her to drop foreign
languages, she just couldn't get the hang of writing in
French, and that freed her up for the extra lessons.
The rest of the time she'd attended all the normal
classes with her friends.

Instead of reading and writing, she now has coaching
in how to study and how to write exam questions.
She's just done her mocks for GCSEs; her predicted
grades are really good: 'As' in design technology and
art, 'Bs' in maths, science and geography and 'Cs' in
English, history and religious studies.

She wants to go on to university and study fashion
design. It's back to Paddington Bear!

What is, and what is not, dyslexia?

Although, historically, dyslexia has been thought of as difficulty with reading, it usually affects all aspects of literacy: reading, spelling and writing.

The problems of someone with dyslexia can sometimes be best illustrated by examining his writing skills. Let's look at a piece of free writing done by a girl called Rebecca (in the box on page 89), when she was asked to write what she had done that morning.

Rebecca

Rebecca is 11 years old and very bright. Her IQ score places her in the top 10 per cent for her age range. For the last six years, skilled teachers have endeavoured to teach her the basics of reading and writing. For a child of her age and IQ, Rebecca has made a lot of errors.

Let's look at two particular errors (circled in red). Rebecca has made errors that are typical of pupils with dyslexia. In the first line, when she started to write the word 'brushed', she used an upper case **B** instead of a lower case **b**. On the third line, she again incorrectly used an upper case **B** rather than a lower case **b**.

After six years of teaching, Rebecca is still having difficulty knowing when and where to use a capital letter correctly and she has used different spellings for the same word even within the space of three lines.

Rebecca's errors are clearly not the errors that you would expect from a pupil of her age and high ability. They are 'age-inappropriate' errors and the presence of such errors is one of the essential elements of a diagnosis of dyslexia.

Michael

Let's now look at a second case study. This is a piece of Michael's writing. He was asked to write about his family (see above).

Two errors are ringed in red. On the first line, Michael has written 'yoostu' where he meant 'used to'. Not only has he misspelt both words, but there is also no space between them. On the bottom line, Michael has written 'cict' for the word kicked.

Now, from these errors it might be easy to assume that Michael is dyslexic, but he is most definitely not! Michael is only six years old and is not dyslexic because he is making 'age-appropriate' errors – ones that are usual for a child of his age.

For example, most teachers would argue that the incorrect spelling 'cict' represents a 'virtuous error' in the sense that Michael clearly recognises every sound in the word and knows a letter that can justly represent that sound.

At Michael's age, this is not incorrect, but shows that his reading and writing are developing normally.

Age-inappropriate errors

In summary, children with dyslexia make age-inappropriate errors in reading and spelling, whereas children who don't have dyslexia may make similar errors but they are generally at a younger age and so their errors are considered to be just part of normal literacy development and therefore age appropriate.

The probable causes of dyslexia

There has been a wide variety of suggestions and hypotheses as to the causes of dyslexia but recent research suggests that a child with dyslexia has

What is and is not dyslexia?

All children have difficulty with writing as they develop their skill. The first example shows the sort of difficulties that a child with dyslexia may have and the second one shows the difficulty often seen in any young child.

1. Rebecca's writing

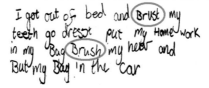

2. Michael's writing

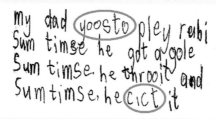

difficulties in one or other (or even both) of the following two areas:

1 Short-term memory, sometimes called working memory

2 Phonological awareness.

Short-term memory difficulties
Research indicates that pupils with dyslexia often also

experience difficulties with a particular aspect of memory called short-term memory. This should not be confused with long-term memory, which is what we usually mean when we talk about 'memory'.

Long-term memory is concerned with things that you remember for a long time, items that seem so 'wired into' your brain that they are always available and easy to access. This might include things such as recalling what you did yesterday, remembering the capital of Italy, the name of the town you were born in and, usually, other things that link with real life and real events.

'Short-term memory' usually refers to your ability to recall a series of unconnected items over a much shorter period of time.

What's it like to have short-term memory difficulty?

The trouble some people have in remembering a new telephone number is a good example of how difficulties in short-term memory affect daily life. Few people would have difficulty remembering a telephone number if the numbers had some obvious association, say 1 2 3 4 5 6, but most numbers (or at least, most telephone numbers) are not linked, and new ones are not easy to remember, even over as short a period as a couple of seconds.

Suppose somebody suggests you telephone me and gives you my number, which is 573192, but you don't have a pencil. To remember the numbers in sequence, you will probably find yourself repeating them over and over in your head (or even aloud) as you walk to the phone.

It is by 'rehearsing' this new information in short-term memory that you are able to remember the sequence of these six unfamiliar and unconnected numbers. If you stop repeating the numbers, even for a few seconds, not only would you forget them, but they would be gone forever – and you would need to be given the numbers again.

What affects short-term memory?
At least two things are important in understanding short-term memory:

1 The need for repetition
2 How many elements (in this case, numbers) can be held in short-term memory.

Clearly, everybody has a limit as to the span or number of items that will fit into their short-term memory: most adults can repeat six or seven unconnected numbers with little difficulty but have trouble with ten numbers. You might start repeating the numbers but, by the time you reached the ninth and tenth numbers, you will probably have forgotten the first numbers, and will not be able to restart the repetition of the series, and so it will be forgotten.

Many people are surprised to learn that short-term memory has little to do with what we commonly think of as 'intelligence': some people who are thought to be highly intelligent may have a short-term memory span of only four or five items, whereas others who might score lower in standard intelligence tests may have a short-term memory span of eight or nine items.

How does short-term memory affect the ability to learn?
To get into long-term memory, to become permanently

and instantly available, strings of unconnected items have to be repeated frequently over a period of time. Some things, like our own or friends' telephone numbers, are used so often and repeated so frequently that they are transferred from short-term memory and appear to become 'wired' into long-term memory, so we have no difficulty recalling them whenever we want.

Many things that we learn are a series of unconnected elements – such as the days of the week, the months of the year, multiplication tables. To illustrate the importance of short-term memory in such tasks, let's look at how children learn the alphabet, a series of 26 unconnected letters.

A young child with a short-term memory, which holds seven items, will progressively learn the alphabet by repeating chunks of seven letters. Another child of the same intelligence, but with a short-term memory that can hold only four items, will learn the alphabet at a much slower pace – in chunks of four letters.

The same happens when learning many of the essential skills necessary for reading, such as the sound that each letter represents or spellings that don't follow the rules. As people with dyslexia have a limited short-term memory span, learning to read is very difficult.

A child with a relatively poor short-term memory will, however, not be unable to learn to read. Learning to read will take him longer and he will inevitably be behind his peer group.

Phonological awareness

Research indicates that many children who have difficulty in acquiring literacy have difficulty with what is known as phonological awareness or the ability to attend to the individual components of sound in speech.

Two important aspects of phonological awareness are:

1 The ability to break up words into their separate sounds: for example, being able to break the word 'cat' into the three sounds, /cuh/ah/tuh/.

2 The ability to blend sounds to make words: knowing that the three sounds /cuh/ah/tuh/ can be blended together to make the word 'cat'.

Many of these skills are easy for people who are not dyslexic but very difficult for people with dyslexia.

Phonological difficulties

Spoken language can be thought to have at least two levels. First, individual words represent individual concepts: for example, the words 'cat', 'mat' and 'sat' each represent identifiable concepts in the real world. Second, these items can be related to form a relational concept: for example, 'the cat sat on the mat'.

All children are, as it were, pre-programmed to learn such concepts almost automatically. All human cultures have spoken language and evolution has made sure that children's brains are specially 'wired' to deal with spoken language.

Written language is different. It has not been around long enough for our brains to be 'wired' to learn to read. How is it different?

Let's analyse a simple question, first as it is spoken and then as it is written. The sentence is:

Would you go?

Say it aloud, two or three times very quickly, and listen to the sounds. Now imagine yourself to be a pre-reading five year old and ask yourself two questions about the way you spoke the sentence:

1 How many words were in the question?

2 What was the last sound of the first word?

If you said these words in the same way that most people speak English, then a five year old listening to you could believe there were only two words, 'wouldyou' and 'go' because, as you said the sentence, you will have merged the first two words in a way that leaves no discernible gap between them.

There is no noticeable space between many of the words in spoken English and, to be able to speak English, you don't need to know much about the spaces between words. However, to read or write English, it is essential to have good knowledge of the spaces between words.

Recognising the individual sounds in speech, knowing that there are spaces between words and knowing where they occur are important aspects of phonological awareness.

Let's turn to the second question. Say the sentence aloud very quickly and then ask yourself: 'What is the last sound of the first word?' You will actually know that the last sound in the first word, 'would' is a /duh/ (that is, the sound represented by the letter **d**) because you have seen it in the printed form, and are able to read it.

However, when speaking the sentence, using the normal English dialect, as demonstrated above, you probably merged the end of the word 'would' into the beginning of the word 'you' so that they sounded like one word 'wouldyou'.

So, the sound you made to end the first word (to the ears of the five year old) is most likely to have been /ju/, rather than a /duh/. Say it again aloud, and listen carefully: /wudju/.

Phonological awareness is the ability not only to recognise but also to separate the sounds within words of the English language – at a simple level, knowing that the word 'cat' can be broken down to make three sounds /cuh/ah/tuh/ and vice versa.

To speak a language, you do not have to have phonological awareness at the level of either recognising spaces between words or hearing the individual sounds within words, but it is important to have phonological awareness to read, spell and write English.

Most children develop phonological awareness easily, whereas children with dyslexia often have difficulty.

KEY POINTS

■ People with dyslexia have difficulty learning to read and write

■ There are thought to be two main factors in specific learning difficulty (dyslexia): difficulties related to short-term memory and difficulties related to phonological awareness

■ A child who has difficulty with literacy skills is likely to have problems in either or both of these areas

■ Neither of these factors is related to intelligence

■ Almost all people with dyslexia eventually learn to read and write, although such tasks may remain hard

■ Schoolchildren with dyslexia often lose self-esteem and come to believe that they are not as clever as others.

Assessment and management of dyslexia

How is dyslexia identified?

It is normally either the parents or a child's teacher who first begins to notice that a child does not appear to be acquiring literacy skills at the same rate as other children of the same age.

Delays in developing literacy skills often become apparent at ages six, seven and eight, although some intelligent children may be able to develop unique strategies that may effectively hide their difficulties for a few more years.

Assessment

However, once a significant delay has been identified, the school, with the agreement of the parents, should ask for an assessment of the child's intellectual abilities and literacy skills. This is normally carried out either by a chartered educational psychologist or by a teacher who has been specially trained in teaching pupils who experience dyslexia.

Assessment of dyslexia will typically be in two phases:

- Phase 1: may require referrals from your family doctor to appropriate professionals for a series of assessments to eliminate:
  - sensory difficulties with hearing and vision
  - significant intellectual and/or learning difficulties
  - spoken language difficulties.

- Phase 2: a comprehensive assessment, requested by the parent via the school or family doctor, by either a chartered educational psychologist and/or a teacher who has been specially trained in teaching pupils who experience dyslexia to determine:
  - the child's general level of intellectual abilities
  - the child's abilities in terms of short-term memory
  - the level of the child's phonological abilities
  - the level of the child's basic literacy skills: for example, sound–letter associations, skills in breaking words into individual sounds and building up words from individual sounds
  - the child's ability in terms of reading accuracy and reading comprehension
  - the child's ability in spelling individual words and in a piece of free composition
  - the child's handwriting skill in terms of accuracy and speed.

How common is it?

Research suggests that as many as 10 per cent of pupils experience dyslexic difficulties ranging from relatively mild to severe. It was assumed, before the year 2000, that more boys than girls had dyslexia but more recent research indicates that girls are just as likely to have dyslexia although, historically, boys have been more likely to 'act out' their frustration and thereby attract teachers' attention more readily.

What can be done to help?

The great majority of children who have dyslexia will be educated in mainstream schools. All children with dyslexia will, however, require some form of support.

How children with dyslexia are best supported during a particular phase of their education depends on a wide range of factors.

Two basic provisions are important throughout the schooling of a child with dyslexia; they are interdependent and both are equally important:

1 Most pupils with dyslexia will be educated in a mainstream school which should have a 'whole school policy' (see page 102 for an explanation) in the way in which pupils with dyslexia are supported.

2 A pupil with dyslexia must be provided with regular, structured, progressive, one-to-one tuition from a teacher trained and experienced in dealing with pupils with dyslexia.

One-to-one specialist tuition

A child with dyslexia must be provided with support from a teacher with formal qualifications and expertise in teaching pupils with dyslexia. Normally, this support is best provided by taking the child out of the classroom for one-to-one or small group teaching for short sessions spread throughout the week.

As is the case with learning many new skills, particularly those that an individual child may find especially difficult, short sessions of twenty minutes, two or three times a week, are normally more effective than one full hour a week. However, one full hour a week is far better than no intervention at all.

As an example, Rebecca, described earlier, would certainly benefit from a full hour of specialist support once a week but is likely to gain more benefit from three sessions of twenty minutes spread throughout the week. The simple ground rule is that 'a little and often' is likely to be more effective than longer periods at greater intervals.

The needs of a pupil with dyslexia are different at each stage of education and what is taught during these sessions varies with each individual pupil.

For example, at age six or seven years, the appropriate focus might be on the development of phonological skills and letter–sound associations. However, at age 14 or 15 years the sessions may be more appropriately focused on how to make notes from textbooks or how to identify the crucial aspects of examination questions, how to plan and write essays, and so on.

In general, research indicates that a child with dyslexia who is still at the stage of acquiring basic literacy skills will benefit most from a programme that does the following:

- Uses a phonological/phonic approach – explicitly teaching letter–sound associations, that is:

  - blending (the ability to 'join' or blend individual sounds to make a word, for example, knowing

that the sounds /cuh/ah/tuh/ can be blended to make the word 'cat')
- segmentation (the ability to 'split' or segment words into separate sounds, for example, knowing that the word 'cat' can be split into the sounds /cuh/ah/tuh/).

- Uses a variety of teaching approaches that engage as many senses as is practicable – speaking, hearing, vision, movement and feeling.

Multisensory techniques for a one-to-one approach

Multisensory teaching techniques incorporate all the above methods and the following simple example illustrates how it is done.

Assume that a child with dyslexia has difficulty learning that the sound /cuh/ (as in cat) is represented by the letter shape 'c'. Instead of the teacher just telling the child, she will be encouraged to do the following:

- Speak the sound /cuh/ aloud with clear articulation.

- Hear the teacher say the sound /cuh/ and then select the corresponding symbol from a selection of letters.

- Say it in response to a 'game' using cards that have:
  - the letter 'c' plus a visual cue – for example, a picture of a cat
  - the letter 'c' with no visual cue.

- Say the sound /cuh/ as she uses movement to trace it in the air or in sand.

- Identify the letter 'c' by feel – as a form of game where the child selects the letter 'c' from a bag filled with a selection of letters cut from sandpaper, or velvet, cardboard, wood, etc.

The basic principle is that, by presenting things to a child in a variety of ways using the full range of senses, the learning is more likely to 'stick'.

In addition, because the child has a poor short-term memory and so requires frequent repetition of tasks that to her seem relatively boring, multisensory approaches enliven the teaching sessions by endless varieties of game-like presentations.

There are a number of published teaching schemes based on these principles. They are presented rather like teaching manuals and those teachers responsible for delivering such programmes must have completed an appropriate course of training.

'Whole school' provision for pupils with dyslexia

Most pupils with dyslexia will and should attend a normal mainstream school and be offered all the subjects of the UK National Curriculum. A very small minority of dyslexic children (less than one per cent) may attend a school that specialises in teaching children who experience 'severe' dyslexic difficulties.

However, whichever school the child attends, it is not enough just to provide one-to-one and/or small group specialist support. There should be a 'whole school policy', which includes at least two major aims:

1 A named teacher is given responsibility for coordinating all the support provided for a pupil with dyslexia. In the UK this is usually the school's Special Educational Needs Coordinator, often abbreviated to SENCO.

2   The school should ensure that all class teachers are offered appropriate training and are aware that the needs of pupils with dyslexia will not be met solely via the provision of one-to-one sessions with a specialist teacher. When a pupil with dyslexia returns to the classroom, responsibility for teaching the child becomes the responsibility of the class teacher.

A whole school policy is aimed at providing a pupil with dyslexia access to a broad and balanced curriculum.

KEY POINTS

■ Most children with dyslexia attend an ordinary school

■ Children with dyslexia need regular and frequent periods of one-to-one or small group tuition

■ The school should have a 'whole school' policy to support them

Dyspraxia

What is dyspraxia?

Dyspraxia or, as it is often known, developmental coordination disorder is an impairment or difficulty in the development of coordinated movement (motor coordination) to a degree that interferes with academic achievement and/or daily living.

Children with dyspraxia are characterised by marked delays in the development of 'motor milestones'. For example, they are slower than other children in learning:

- to sit, crawl, walk
- to develop ball skills and other sport-related activities
- to master coordinated skills such as riding a bicycle
- to achieve fluent, legible handwriting.

A child with dyspraxia experiences difficulty learning such skills to a degree that is significantly greater than would be expected for other children of a similar age.

Case study: Christopher

Christopher is seven now, and just about to start junior school. We've always been worried about him, nothing you could put your finger on, just vague things that didn't seem quite right.

I still remember, as he was rushed out of the delivery room, one of the hospital staff whispering on the internal phone that Christopher had 'breathing difficulties'. As it turned out he was in an incubator for two weeks.

His weight had dropped in the first week and he was fed using a nasogastric tube but, after about two weeks, he came out of the incubator and we tried to feed him using a bottle. Trouble was he seemed only able to take small amounts, so little that I had to feed him every two or three hours.

As a baby he wasn't like his brother. Christopher always seemed to be irritable, constantly crying. The only time he seemed to stop was when he was being carried and rocked or was in his carrycot in the car.

During his first year, things sometimes got so bad that either his dad or I resorted to taking him out in the car just so we could get some peace!

He seemed to be much slower than his brother at things like sitting and walking, and he never crawled, just seemed to leave that out completely. He sort of bum-shuffled by pushing himself along on his bottom with his legs. I remember how he liked being in the kitchen, because he could push himself around on the shiny floor, which he couldn't do on the lounge carpet.

His brother had been walking by about 11 months but Christopher didn't learn until way past his second birthday. Feeding him was a nightmare; up till the age of three I had to liquidise everything; anything solid and he just spat it out, almost like he couldn't chew.

'The only time he seemed to stop crying was when he was being carried or rocked or was in his carrycot in the car.'

In some areas he seemed much quicker than other children. He was able to respond to his name at about eight months, much quicker than his brother, and he recognised family relatives and friends by smiling or reaching out to them well before the age of ten months.

By 18 months he was fascinated by children's books and when I turned the pages of his favourite book he was even able, without me prompting him, to make the sounds of the animals like 'moo' for the cow and 'hee-haw' for the donkey.

Even though he obviously loved the book, by the age of two years he still couldn't turn the pages by himself, just couldn't seem to master the business of

'In some areas he seemed much quicker than other children – by 18 months he was fascinated by children's books.'

using his thumb and forefinger to grip a single page and then turn it.

At age three and four, he seemed to have little difficulty in understanding what was said to him, but often seemed to have great difficulty speaking clearly. His brother and I were sometimes the only people able to understand what he was saying. Even his dad had difficulty.

Words were often jumbled, such as when he wanted a particular children's video he might ask for 'Builder the Bob' or when trying to say long words like spaghetti or elephant they would come out as 'pasgetti' or 'ephelant'.

It was when he went to nursery school that I began to notice big differences between Christopher and the other children. Alongside other children he looked awkward. When he walked, his gait looked unbalanced, like a much younger child, especially if he was in a hurry to do something, or excited.

He was always bumping into the other children or tripping over things. Even at the age of four to five years he always had to be taken to the toilet, because he still couldn't pull his trousers up and down properly by himself.

This became more and more of a problem because he began to get upset about going to the toilet in the nursery, and for a long time would only use the toilet at home. He never used climbing frames and often ended up crying and frozen to the spot even when on just the second or third rung of the ladder on the slide in the playground.

Every time all the children went out into the playground or it was time to go home, one of the nursery staff always had to help Christopher put on his coat. At home and in shops, he always walked downstairs sideways, one step at a time. Getting on and off escalators is still a problem and, remember, he's seven now.

He's still always dropping things, knocking over cups, leaving food spread all around his plate. He has never seemed to be able to control a pencil as well as other children of his age; he never enjoyed colouring or scribbling games.

At school, unless they force him, he refuses to join in any activities involving pens, coloured pencils, paintbrushes or anything like that.

'He never used climbing frames and would freeze on the spot when only on the second or third rung of the ladder on the slide in the playground.'

He never seems to like being in the company of other children. The funny thing is he has always really liked being with adults; even at school he still often ends up trailing around behind the teachers at play time.

They like his company and tell me he often says things, and knows things, well in advance of his age. The most frequent phrase I hear his teachers say about him is: 'He's a right little puzzle isn't he?'

As with many developmental disorders, the needs of a pupil with dyspraxia are different at each stage of education. This is well illustrated by David's mother's story.

Case study: David

David is aged 12 years, just finishing his first year at secondary school. He's come to hate going to school, some mornings even pretending to be ill to try to get out of going.

It's really strange in some ways, because he's a bit of a bookworm and spends most of his time reading, mainly factual books. At the moment he reads everything he can about the life of sea animals such as sharks, whales, sea lions, dolphins, etc.

Although he reads a lot, he gets low marks for almost everything he does at school, mainly because his handwriting is terrible. I remember when he was in the infants and early years of the junior school, he

'Although David reads a lot, he gets low marks for almost everything he does at school, mainly because his handwriting is awful.'

tried very hard at his writing, but he's now all but given up. On some days he can't even write his name legibly.

Oddly enough his spelling is pretty good, but only if you ask him to spell it out by saying the letters. Ask him to write it down and you won't be able to read it. It's not just that individual letters are the wrong shape, he often writes letters in words so they overlap and very often he can't keep letters on a line.

He's even been known to keep writing until his pen slips off the edge of the page. In his school books, the first few lines of an exercise might be just legible but the rest of it will be a complete mess.

All his schoolbooks look like they've been written in by someone who has no persistence, loses interest quickly, doesn't care, is lazy and not very bright. When he's asked to write something nobody can read it and, more often than not, he can't even read it himself.

In class his teachers say he answers questions better than most of the other kids; everybody knows he's clever. But ask him to write anything down and it's hopeless, completely illegible.

A lot of his teachers in the secondary school, particularly those who only see him once or twice a week, simply think he's not trying very hard. But I've seen him crying at home just trying to get his homework done, particularly when he's interested in the subject.

A lot of his teachers give him low marks all the time; they cover his exercise books with comments that are different ways of saying 'must try harder'.

It's a bit of a self-fulfilling prophecy in the sense that, when it comes to writing or homework, David does everything he can to get out of it, delay it or finish it quickly with the minimum effort. Now he's in

'A lot of his teachers simply think he's not trying very hard, but I've seen him crying at home trying to get his work done.'

secondary school, his teachers' comments, sadly, contain more than just a grain of truth.

When he's writing, David looks awkward, even the way he sits. He looks tense, his feet are often crossed, sometimes seeming to even grip one of the chair legs. He holds the pencil almost in his fist, rather than his fingers, and seems to literally ram it into the paper.

When he was younger, he tried so hard that he sometimes bit his lip until it bled but he hasn't tried that hard in a long time. Not since he realised that no matter how hard he tried, his writing was always bad. His classmates took to calling him 'geek'.

David has always been the last into and out of the school changing rooms. In the junior school he once put his football boots on the wrong feet, a mistake that one of the other boys noticed in the middle of a game and pointed out to everybody else in a loud, clear voice. David ran off the field in tears and the teacher had to coax him out of the toilet cubicle where he'd locked himself.

When David leaves a changing room after a game or at the swimming pool, his shirt buttons are often done up in the wrong order, his shoe laces undone and he's long since given up trying to reknot his school tie. He acutely feels this loss of face to a degree where he has taken to forging his own 'sick notes' to get out of games and swimming.

In the school playground, David never tries to play with other children. He always seems to be hovering

'When David leaves the changing room, his shirt buttons are often done up in the wrong order and he has long since given up trying to re-knot his school tie.'

on the outskirts of any game or a crowd of boys, sort of present but not playing or being part of the group.

He used to try to join in but when they picked teams, he was always the last to be chosen, and often even that was after a loud discussion among the better players as to which side should be 'handicapped' by having David in their team.

Outside school, David does not join in with other children because he can't really ride a bike or use a skateboard, at least not like the other kids. When he's on a skateboard, he's a positive danger to himself and other people.

When he was nine we took him on a skiing holiday but he spent almost every day in tears of frustration on the nursery slopes, pretending to be injured or, on the last day, refusing to leave the hotel room.

In conversation with adults, though, David is a different boy: quick-witted and clever. In his efforts to gain popularity with his peer group, he often misjudges how caustic some of his comments can be and some of the targets of his humour strike back, physically.

It is difficult to judge whether this is bullying because in the inevitable 'he-said-I-said' enquiry by teachers or us, David has often had to admit that some remark he's made, although both clever and funny to everybody else, is often very upsetting to the person on the receiving end.

As parents, we are becoming worried that he's now almost isolated among his peer group. He rarely leaves the house after school and seems to have no real friends. He tends to spend his life curled up with a book or watching videos on his own.

'As parents we are becoming worried that he's now almost isolated among his peer group.'

Only this month, I've twice found him crying in his room. When I ask him why he just says, 'I'm a useless geek' but won't explain further.

Diagnosis of dyspraxia

If you think that your child shows signs of dyspraxia, the first step is to contact your family doctor who may refer your child to an appropriately qualified medical professional, usually a paediatrician and/or an occupational therapist.

You should consult your doctor if you can tick more than three of the aspects of your child's development in the box on page 116.

Diagnosis of dyspraxia

The following is a list of the features commonly seen in a child with dyspraxia. You can use it to see if you should seek further advice from your GP.

Tick the box if your child:

☐ Was slow to develop early 'motor' milestones – for example, sitting up, crawling, walking

☐ Was slow to develop age-appropriate eating skills – such as using a knife and fork

☐ Tended to be more wary and timid on children's climbing apparatus than other children

☐ Was slow in developing age-appropriate ball skills

☐ Had difficulty learning to ride a bicycle

☐ Constantly stumbled into furniture, knocked things over, was generally clumsy

☐ Required help with dressing skills for longer than his peer group

☐ Has hand-writing skills that have been consistently worse than those of his peer group

Causes, incidence and long-term consequences of dyspraxia
Causes

The exact causes of dyspraxia are not yet fully understood. It is thought to be underpinned by poor or slow development of those areas of the brain involved in performing sequences of coordinated muscle movements (motor movements), for example, the coordination required in catching and throwing a ball, riding a bicycle, using a computer 'mouse' and handwriting.

There is no good research evidence to suggest that it is caused by environmental factors such as poor diet, pollution or immunisations.

Incidence

During the past decade, developmental dyspraxia has come to be known as the 'hidden handicap' because it is often more difficult to diagnose than many of the other disorders of childhood. Developmental dyspraxia affects between two and five per cent of the population with a ratio of four boys to every girl.

Long-term consequences

There is general consensus that dyspraxia is a life-long condition. There is no research that shows that it can be 'cured'. However, evidence from many clinicians and parents shows that early therapy reduces the levels of distress caused by many of the symptoms.

After adolescence, movement difficulties become less problematic, if only because, as an individual matures, he becomes more able to cope. For example, after schooling, the individual can 'choose' whether or not to take part in particular sports and avoid, or at least limit, his need to engage in tasks that require a particularly high degree of coordination.

However, anecdotal biographical evidence suggests that it is not unusual for someone with dyspraxia to continue to show a range of emotional problems, such as low self-esteem, into adulthood. This seems to come from living a childhood in which he came to believe that he was 'poor at almost everything'.

What is it like to have dyspraxia?

One way of explaining this to an adult who has no difficulties in motor planning is to describe the motor movements involved in a relatively common event such as picking up a wine glass when being offered a drink.

Using motor planning to pick up a wine glass

Imagine you are at a party and that in front of you is a tray of wine glasses standing, as is often the case, upside down (with the stems uppermost). Now assume that your host is walking towards you with a bottle of wine and offers you a drink, which you accept. Just think through what usually happens as you pick up the wine glass.

If you're right-handed, you'll use this arm and hand to reach towards the stem of one of the wine glasses. Most people will then rotate their right arm and wrist anticlockwise until the hand is almost upside down before pinching the stem of one of the wine glasses between the finger and thumb.

Then, as the glass is lifted, the wrist is turned clockwise in a smooth movement. This ensures that, by the time the movement is finished, the glass is in an upright position ready for the wine to be poured.

The whole action is completed in one smooth movement, all of which is planned automatically and without conscious thought as you first reached for the glass. It is unlikely that anybody taught you how to do this – you do it naturally.

But think it through again and, if you can, try it with a wine glass. The movement is actually very awkward at the start. You turn your wrist right over.

However, this is because you are adept at motor planning. You automatically knew the best lifting action to make sure that the glass was in the correct position when it came to pouring the drink. You do not have a motor planning difficulty.

What would that be like if you had dyspraxia?

A person with dyspraxia finds such motor planning difficult. It does not necessarily mean that he will drop the glass or even look terribly awkward. The likelihood is, however, that the person with dyspraxia will first pick up the glass in one hand, then use both hands to turn it over, before holding it out with one hand ready for the drink to be poured.

How your motor planning is affected by your skill level

This might seem a very rare example of motor planning using a task that doesn't happen very often, unless of course you go to a lot of parties! But let's take another example.

Imagine the day that you passed your driving test. Immediately after you had passed your driving test, if a friend had been in the car with you the likelihood is that your friend would have looked at your driving and commented on how good it was.

For example, before pulling away from the kerb-side, because these things were fresh in your mind, you would have looked in the mirror, let off the handbrake, operated the indicator, placed the car in gear and moved slowly and safely away. For the next few miles your friend would have been impressed with your driving skill.

Now imagine that your friend had then begun to engage you in a deep conversation that required you to think. Eventually you would probably have told your friend, possibly in an exasperated voice, to be quiet because you needed to focus on your driving.

This would have been because, at that time, your driving skill was in a state where you needed to think about the movements that you were making. Listening and responding to your friend would simply have got in the way.

There is no doubt that, if you have been driving for a few years, you can now drive automatically in the sense that you have no difficulty carrying on a conversation and moving the steering wheel appropriately while at the same time manipulating the clutch, gears and accelerator, noticing the cyclist behind you, the bus in front beginning to pull out and the traffic lights changing 50 metres ahead.

What would that be like if you had dyspraxia?

A person with dyspraxia may learn to drive, and be able to drive perfectly safely, but may not perform driving actions completely automatically. So as an example, an adult with dyspraxia may not feel comfortable talking and driving.

How are other tasks affected?

Now think about the many skilled planned movements that you make every day: doing up shoelaces, washing and drying up dishes, ironing clothes, manipulating pots and pans while cooking. The magic is that most of us can do these tasks automatically, even while we are thinking of something else.

The likelihood is that an adult with dyspraxia will also be able to do all these tasks, but has to think about it, focusing on it rather more than we do.

If he is in a conversation or thinking about something else, it is at that point that he is likely to make a mistake.

What's it like for a child with dyspraxia?

Now transfer this kind of thinking to a child with dyspraxia:

- A seven year old won't be able to do up the laces on a pair of trainers while at the same time talking to other people in the changing room.

- A nine year old may not be able to pour milk from a carton into a glass while at the same time watching a video.

- A twelve year old won't be able to write legibly when answering an exam question while worrying about the time limit.

It's hard to do two things at once

People with dyspraxia have difficulty with motor planning, which means that they may learn to perform a task *effectively* but may still have difficulty performing the task *automatically*. To put it in cartoon form: a person with dyspraxia can walk and talk – but if walking down a street and talking at the same time, may walk into a lamp post!

The difficulty with motor planning for a person with dyspraxia pervades almost every aspect of everyday life.

KEY POINTS

- The causes of dyspraxia are unknown

- Approximately five to seven per cent of children are dyspraxic with a boy to girl ratio of four to one

- Children with dyspraxia are slow to develop motor milestones – for example, sitting up, crawling, running

- Children with dyspraxia have difficulty planning motor movements – for example, difficulties with dressing skills, ball skills and handwriting

- Children with dyspraxia often lack self-esteem

- Children and adults with dyspraxia often have difficulty doing two things at once – finding it hard to combine physical activity with a task requiring thought

Assessment and management of dyspraxia

What can be done to help?

There are no drugs to treat dyspraxia. Treatment is almost always in the form of exercises under the guidance of an occupational therapist, who is a medically trained professional with expertise in diagnosing developmental coordination disorder (dyspraxia) and in developing individual treatment plans.

Normally, your family doctor will initiate referral to an occupational therapist.

What is the treatment like?

Treatment usually involves regular meetings with the therapist (often weekly or monthly).

In the intervals between appointments the child, under the guidance of an adult, will be required to practise a range of tasks, advised by the occupational therapist, as appropriate for a particular child at a specific time in his development.

It is not possible to provide a comprehensive description of therapy but examples may be helpful. The exercises described below are typical of those used at different stages of childhood development.

Typical exercises

The regime of exercises will clearly be more effective if the home and school cooperate in ensuring that the child practises the exercises on a regular basis.

In nursery and infant classes, the child with dyspraxia may complete obstacle courses, which involve large body movements such as crawling, creeping and climbing over children's playground equipment.

In early junior school, he may be asked to practise walking on a balance beam positioned just a few inches above the floor or to perform heel–toe walking. He may take part in activities that demand jumping off play equipment while at the same time turning in the air. As a classroom activity, he may be asked to practise fine motor movements such as using a pair of scissors or threading beads while being timed.

At the later junior level, he might be asked to practise catching skills using a bean bag – because it wraps round the hand rather than bouncing off. In the classroom, he may be asked to perform tasks that develop fine motor skills by using construction toys – such as Lego or sewing/tapestry.

At the start of secondary school, the activities may well turn away from practising motor activities to focus on organisational skills such as how to develop and use 'to-do' lists, diaries and timetables.

Little and often

It is difficult to be prescriptive in terms of the frequency and the length of these practice sessions, and the occupational therapist will advise. However, as with learning almost any skilled task, 'a little and often' will usually be more effective than longer sessions at greater intervals.

To illustrate this point, if the child is required to practise tasks such as tying shoelaces or fastening buttons, then, clearly, three short 10-minute sessions spread throughout each day are likely to be more effective than two 75-minute sessions per week.

Fun

Another important factor in developing a programme of exercises is to ensure that the exercises are 'fun', which is usually achieved by designing activities where the child can practise the required tasks as integral parts of a game.

Help with exams

The child with dyspraxia will usually experience difficulty with handwriting, legibility and speed, which becomes more important as he approaches formal school examinations, that is, at ages 15 to 18.

So, at this time he may benefit from support with basic study skills – such as taking notes, writing essays, and planning and writing examination answers.

At this age, he may need to learn typing and word-processing skills and may also benefit from the use of speech-to-text software – where he speaks into a microphone and the computer types the words as text.

Help with self-esteem

The above should give a sense of how a child with dyspraxia may be supported at different ages. His difficulties with tasks requiring muscular coordination should always be handled with sensitivity and tact but, in addition, he is likely to need support to bolster his self-esteem.

This can often be achieved simply through ensuring that both the child's parents and the child's teachers understand the difficulties that he experiences and sensitively provide him with self-knowledge on the nature of his own difficulties.

KEY POINTS

■ Dyspraxia cannot be cured but therapy in the form of exercises will help – as difficulties often decrease with appropriate support and maturity, the earlier the intervention the better

■ It is important to remember that it is not the case that children with dyspraxia will not learn tasks requiring coordination; the important issue is that they will often require more practice than their age-related peers

Useful information

Where can I find out more?

We have included the following organisations because, on preliminary investigation, they may be of use to the reader. However, we do not have first-hand experience of each organisation and so cannot guarantee the organisation's integrity. The reader must therefore exercise his or her own discretion and judgement when making further enquiries.

Attention deficit hyperactivity disorder

Attention Deficit Disorder Information and Support Service (ADDISS)
10 Station Road, Mill Hill
London NW7 2JU
Tel: 020 8906 9068
Fax: 020 8959 0727
Email: info@addiss.co.uk
Website: www.addiss.co.uk

Offers information about and resources for ADHD and associated conditions to parents, sufferers, teachers and health professionals.

Autistic spectrum disorders

Aspen UK (Asperger's Syndrome Professional Support Network)
Castle Heights, 2nd Floor, 72 Maid Marion Way
Nottingham NG1 6BJ
Tel: 0115 911 3360
Email: abicknell@nas.org.uk
Website: www.nas.org.uk

Professionals from diverse disciplines coming together to offer support and information to professionals working with people suffering from Asperger's syndrome and develop services.

National Autistic Society (NAS)
393 City Road
London EC1V 1NG
Tel: 020 7833 2299
Fax: 020 7833 9666
Helpline: 0845 070 4004
Email: nas@nas.org.uk
Website: www.nas.org.uk

Champions the interests of all people with autism and Asperger's syndrome. Offers information and a wide range of support to individuals, their families and professionals working with them. The Centre for Social and Communications Disorders provides a complete diagnostic assessment and advice service throughout the UK and training courses for professionals. A wide range of residential and day services available.

PARIS (Public Autism Resource and Information Service)
Online service by NAS offers workshops for parents, seminars and organises care/holiday schemes. Local branches have support groups.

Dyslexia
British Dyslexia Association (BDA)
98 London Road, Reading RG1 5AU
Tel: 0118 966 2677
Fax: 0118 935 1927
Helpline: 0118 966 8271
Email: helpline@bdadyslexia.org.uk
Website: www.bdadyslexia.org.uk

Represents people with dyslexia and promotes early identification and support in schools to ensure opportunities to learn for pupils with dyslexia. Offers information and advice to schools and the workplace. Has local groups around the UK.

Dyspraxia
Dyscovery Centre
Alltyryn Campus, University of Wales
Newport NP20 5DA
Tel: 01633 432330
Fax: 01633 432331
Email: dyscovery.centre@newport.ac.uk
Website: www.dyscovery.co.uk

Provides a service with interdisciplinary team helping individuals with living and learning difficulties. Offers assessment, training and education courses for the public and professionals.

All developmental disorders
Aspire Consulting Psychologists
10 Harley Street
London W1G 9PF or
The Manor Hospital
Oxford OX3 7RP or
The Nuffield Hospital
Cheltenham GL51 6SY
Tel/Fax: 01242 574646
Email: office@aspirepsychologists.co.uk
Website: www.aspirepsychlogists.co.uk

Educational psychologists in private practice offering assessments for pupils and adults who may show signs of giftedness or general and specific learning difficulties. Provide in-service training for teachers, psychologists, education, and health and social service professionals and parents. Appear as expert witness at educational tribunals and court cases.

Other useful addresses
Benefits Enquiry Line
Tel: 0800 882200
Minicom: 0800 243355
Website: www.dwp.gov.uk
N. Ireland:
Tel: 0800 220674
Minicom: 0800 243789

Government agency giving information and advice on sickness and disability benefits for people with disability and their carers.

Carers UK
20–25 Glasshouse Yard
London EC1A 4JT
Tel: 020 7490 8818
Fax: 020 7490 8824
Helpline: 0808 808 7777 (Wed, Thurs 10am–12 noon;
2–4pm)
Email: info@ukcarers.org
Website: www.carersonline.org.uk

Offers information, support and advice on the
practical, financial and emotional aspects of being a
carer through a network of local branches.

Citizens Advice Bureaux
Myddleton House, 115–123 Pentonville Road
London N1 9LZ
Tel: 020 7833 2181 (admin only)
Website: www.adviceguide.org.uk

HQ of national charity offering a wide variety of
practical, financial and legal advice. Network of local
charities throughout the UK listed in phone books and
in *Yellow Pages* under 'C'.

NHS Direct
Tel: 0845 4647 (24 hours, 365 days a year)
Textphone: 0845 606 4647
Website: www.nhsdirect.nhs.uk
NHS Scotland: 0800 224 88

Offers confidential health-care advice, information and
referral service. A good first port of call for any health
advice.

National Institute for Health and Clinical Excellence (NICE)
MidCity Place, 71 High Holborn
London WC1V 6NA
Tel: 020 7067 5800
Fax: 020 7067 5801
Email: nice@nice.org.uk
Website: www.nice.org.uk

Provides national guidance on the promotion of good health and the prevention and treatment of ill-health. Patient information leaflets are available for each piece of guidance issued.

Prodigy Website
Sowerby Centre for Health Informatics at Newcastle (SCHIN), Bede House, All Saints Business Centre
Newcastle upon Tyne NE1 2ES
Tel: 0191 243 6100
Fax: 0191 243 6101
Email: prodigy-enquiries@schin.co.uk
Website: www.prodigy.nhs.uk

A website mainly for GPs giving information for patients listed by disease plus named self-help organisations.

The internet as a further source of information

After reading this book, you may feel that you would like further information on the subject. The internet is of course an excellent place to look and there are many websites with useful information about medical disorders, related charities and support groups.

For those who do not have a computer at home some bars and cafes offer facilities for accessing the internet. These are listed in the *Yellow Pages* under 'Internet Bars and Cafes' and 'Internet Providers'. Your local library offers a similar facility and has staff to help you find the information that you need.

It should always be remembered, however, that the internet is unregulated and anyone is free to set up a website and add information to it. Many websites offer impartial advice and information that has been compiled and checked by qualified medical professionals. Some, on the other hand, are run by commercial organisations with the purpose of promoting their own products. Others still are run by pressure groups, some of which will provide carefully assessed and accurate information whereas others may be suggesting medications or treatments that are not supported by the medical and scientific community.

Unless you know the address of the website you want to visit – for example, www.familydoctor.co.uk – you may find the following guidelines useful when searching the internet for information.

Search engines and other searchable sites

Google (www.google.co.uk) is the most popular search engine used in the UK, followed by Yahoo! (http://uk.yahoo.com) and MSN (www.msn.co.uk). Also popular are the search engines provided by Internet Service Providers such as Tiscali and other sites such as the BBC site (www.bbc.co.uk).

In addition to the search engines that index the whole web, there are also medical sites with search facilities, which act almost like mini-search engines, but cover only medical topics or even a particular area of medicine. Again, it is wise to look at who is responsible for compiling the information offered to ensure that it is impartial and medically accurate. The NHS Direct site (www.nhsdirect.nhs.uk) is an example of a searchable medical site.

Links to many British medical charities can be found at the Association of Medical Research Charities' website (www.amrc.org.uk) and at Charity Choice (www.charitychoice.co.uk).

Search phrases

Be specific when entering a search phrase. Searching for information on 'cancer' will return results for many different types of cancer as well as on cancer in general. You may even find sites offering astrological information. More useful results will be returned by using search phrases such as 'lung cancer' and 'treatments for lung cancer'. Both Google and Yahoo! offer an advanced search option that includes the ability to search for the exact phrase, enclosing the search phrase in quotes, that is, 'treatments for lung cancer' will have the same effect. Limiting a search to an exact phrase reduces the number of results returned but it is best to refine a search to an exact match only if you are not getting useful results with a normal search. Adding 'UK' to your search term will bring up mainly British sites, so a good phrase might be 'lung cancer' UK (don't include UK within the quotes).

Always remember the internet is international and unregulated. It holds a wealth of valuable information but individual sites may be biased, out of date or just plain wrong. Family Doctor Publications accepts no responsibility for the content of links published in this series.

Index

Your pages

We have included the following pages because they may help you manage your illness or condition and its treatment.

Before an appointment with a health professional, it can be useful to write down a short list of questions of things that you do not understand, so that you can make sure that you do not forget anything.

Some of the sections may not be relevant to your circumstances.

We are always pleased to receive constructive criticism or suggestions about how to improve the books. You can contact us at:

Email: familydoctor@btinternet.com
Letter: Family Doctor Publications
         PO Box 4664
         Poole
         BH15 1NN

Thank you

Health-care contact details

Name:

Job title:

Place of work:

Tel:

Name:

Job title:

Place of work:

Tel:

Name:

Job title:

Place of work:

Tel:

Name:

Job title:

Place of work:

Tel:

**Significant past health events – illnesses/
operations/investigations/treatments**

Event	Month	Year	Age (at time)

Appointments for health care

Name:

Place:

Date:

Time:

Tel:

Name:

Place:

Date:

Time:

Tel:

Name:

Place:

Date:

Time:

Tel:

Name:

Place:

Date:

Time:

Tel:

Appointments for health care

Name:

Place:

Date:

Time:

Tel:

Name:

Place:

Date:

Time:

Tel:

Name:

Place:

Date:

Time:

Tel:

Name:

Place:

Date:

Time:

Tel:

Current medication(s) prescribed by your doctor

Medicine name:

Purpose:

Frequency & dose:

Start date:

End date:

Medicine name:

Purpose:

Frequency & dose:

Start date:

End date:

Medicine name:

Purpose:

Frequency & dose:

Start date:

End date:

Medicine name:

Purpose:

Frequency & dose:

Start date:

End date:

Other medicines/supplements you are taking, not prescribed by your doctor

Medicine/treatment:

Purpose:

Frequency & dose:

Start date:

End date:

Medicine/treatment:

Purpose:

Frequency & dose:

Start date:

End date:

Medicine/treatment:

Purpose:

Frequency & dose:

Start date:

End date:

Medicine/treatment:

Purpose:

Frequency & dose:

Start date:

End date:

Questions to ask at appointments
(Note: do bear in mind that doctors work under great time pressure, so long lists may not be helpful for either of you)

Questions to ask at appointments

(Note: do bear in mind that doctors work under great time
pressure, so long lists may not be helpful for either of you)

Notes

Notes

Notes

Notes

Notes

Notes

Notes